LIVING WITH

ADD

A Workbook for Adults with Attention Deficit Disorder

M. Susan Roberts, Ph.D.
Gerard J. Jansen, Ph.D.

New Harbinger Publications

Distributed in Canada by Raincoast Books.

Copyright © 1997 by M. Susan Roberts, Ph.D., and Gerard J. Jansen, Ph.D.
New Harbinger Publications, Inc.
5674 Shattuck Avenue
Oakland, CA 94609

Cover design and illustration by Lightbourne Images © 1996.
Text design by Tracy Marie Powell.

Library of Congress Catalog Card Number: 96-71152
ISBN 1-57224-063-6 paperback

New Harbinger Publications' Web site address: www.newharbinger.com

07   06   05

20   19   18   17   16   15   14

We want to thank family, friends, and colleagues who have contributed ideas, experiences, and invaluable information for this book. We are grateful to Frank Quinn who provided encouragement, enthusiasm, and reference material. Thanks also to Joan and Ed Smith for their feedback and ideas. Finally, we want to thank Joanne Bayliss for helpful reference material and suggestions for content areas.

To John,
In anticipation of the adventures to come.

Contents

1

Introduction

Living with Attention Deficit Disorder (ADD) can feel like you're driving down a steep hill at full speed—in a car without brakes. Some moments are exciting—even exhilarating. As you take the bends and curves, you're never sure what's coming next. Other moments are sheer panic. You feel out of control and don't know what to do about it.

ADD is not new, but recognition of it as a distinct disorder is. There is a great deal of current interest in ADD, and our knowledge is advancing by leaps and bounds. We know now that the basis of ADD is neurological. It's not a character flaw. It's not a problem that you'll outgrow if you just try hard enough. ADD affects all aspects of adult life. It affects personal and family relationships and how you feel about yourself. It affects career choices, finances, and opportunity.

The mind of a person with ADD is an active place to be. Sensations are coming in from all sides, and ideas are bouncing off in all directions. A person with ADD may be imaginative, inventive, and downright creative. But much of the time, an ADDer is stymied by disorganization, procrastination, and a persistent sense of being overwhelmed. Our increasing knowledge of ADD is being translated into improved treatment. So, there is much to be learned, and there is reason for hope.

Kurt, 38, presents a common experience with ADD. With treatment, he is becoming more comfortable and productive with ADD. Diagnosed at age 30, Kurt's signs of ADD appeared in early childhood. Kurt had broken a leg and both arms by the age of 10. He was always on the move: climbing, bike riding, and especially, running. He could not sit still in school, talked out of turn, and did poorly in anything requiring accuracy. If the teacher's back was turned for a minute, Kurt was out of his seat—dancing in the aisles. Being the class clown, his classmates loved him until his temper let loose. If he could not hit a home run, he might throw down his bat and quit the game or start a fight. He often said cruel things to other children. He was really trying to be funny and could not understand their resentment.

Kurt started college and enjoyed the social life immensely. But after taking an incomplete in every single class, he dropped out. A friend was opening a bicycle shop, and Kurt took a job in sales. He was great. His charm and enthusiasm made him the top salesperson month after month. He was promoted to management, and that's when the trouble began. Kurt couldn't get organized. He lost memos and reports. His work schedules were always late. Kurt was frustrated and embarrassed. He hid his shame in angry outbursts. He finally had to leave. The next ten years repeated this pattern of first excelling and then failing over and over. He didn't marry. He changed girlfriends as often as he did jobs. His relationships were volatile, with much arguing and passion.

After a string of drunk-driving charges, Kurt lost his driver's license. He was sentenced to mandatory rehabilitation. A counselor recognized his symptoms and diagnosed ADD. Kurt is now taking medication, reading everything he can get his hands on about ADD, and regularly attending a support group. He has returned to a position in sales, which is what he really likes. He feels focused, finally. There are down days when he mourns the lost years, but he's working on forgiving his family, teachers, and himself.

A Brief History of ADD

Although ADD is receiving a lot of attention lately, it has always been a part of human nature. ADD is not the result of high-sugar diets, excessive exposure to fast-paced TV, or permissive parenting, as some have speculated. Children have always been inattentive, impulsive, and hyperactive; putting their teachers and parents to the test. What is new about ADD is our increasing understanding of its nature and promise for treatment.

The first seventy years of research and writing were devoted to ADD in childhood and reflected a primary concern with hyperactivity. (It is, after all, the squeaky wheel that gets the grease.) Clinicians through the years consistently sought a biological basis for hyperactivity. Blaming parenting styles, luckily, has not been a major distraction for researchers in the field.

Early thinking assumed that hyperactive children outgrew ADD. This presumption is natural, as the focus was on hyperactivity, which does diminish with age. Not until the 1980s did clinicians realize that problems maintaining attention did not go away. Today we know that ADD continues throughout the life span. Eighty percent of children with ADD continue to warrant the diagnosis in adulthood.

The Basics of ADD

ADD makes it difficult to regulate attention and to control impulses. ADD is a biological fact of life. It is no more anyone's fault than being born with an irregular heartbeat or large feet. ADD has been likened to nearsightedness. Without corrective lenses, it can distort everything you see and then do.

ADD Can Be Inherited

ADD may be passed from either the mother or father, and it sometimes skips a generation. Support for the genetic nature of ADD is found in studies of twins. We know that identical twins have a much higher incidence of ADD than fraternal twins. Russell Barkley, a leading authority on ADD, reports that it may be the most inherited of all psychiatric disorders. Joseph Biederman, another ADD expert, reports that 30 percent of children with hyperactivity have at least one parent with ADD.

ADD Is a Neurological Condition

Support for the neurological basis of ADD first came in 1990 as a result of work by Alan Zametkin of the National Institute of Mental Health. Results of brain scans revealed that the frontal lobes of persons with ADD had a decreased blood flow and decreased use of glucose (brain fuel), which is carried in the blood. If the frontal lobes can't adequately use glucose, their job of initiating behavior and regulating impulses can be impaired. Daniel Amen, using other brain-scan techniques, discovered that the ADDer's brain functions normally until it tries to concentrate, and then blood flow decreases as does available glucose. Other brain-based findings have contributed to our understanding of ADD as a biological disorder. The *candate nucleus* (sitting deep in the middle of the brain), has a smaller left side and decreased blood flow in people with ADD. The job of the *candate nucleus* is to initiate and inhibit movement and attention and then pass these messages to the frontal lobes where final decisions are made. H. C. Low found that the blood flow of this midbrain section is normal when Ritalin is taken. Finally, some sections of the corpus callosum are smaller in children with ADD. The *corpus callosum* connects the left half of the brain to the right half and is responsible for a great deal of communication between the halves. Problems with the *corpus callosum* may be the reason people with ADD cannot verbalize (left-side brain function) their innovative ideas (right-side brain function).

Our understanding of the nature of ADD is growing. As more information becomes available, it is likely that we will find subtypes of ADD based on specific neurological causes, resulting in improved diagnosis and treatment.

ADD makes it difficult for you to slow down or speed up when needed. It is primarily a problem of inhibiting impulses to say what is on your mind or to do what you are thinking *right now*. It is also characterized by problems regulating energy levels and attention when you want to. While people with ADD are as varied from one another in size, shape, age, and tastes as all other people, they do have problems regulating their behavior in three primary areas: attention, hyperactivity, and impulsivity.

Attention

Problems with attention are so central, that even the name for ADD is derived from it. But in many ways attention deficit disorder is a misnomer. Many think of ADD as synonymous with short attention span, thoughts jumping from topic to topic, and an inability to focus on any one topic. But people with ADD can attend to a task for long periods of time. ADDers even have the special ability to hyperfocus. They can concentrate with complete and satisfied absorption when the task is novel and interesting to them.

> Jane, a 44-year-old office manager, has difficulty maintaining attention to task. As a result, she shifts from task to task in a way that leaves her office workers dazed. She will plow through a catalog for new computer equipment for five to ten minutes; stop suddenly and turn to writing a memo for a new position she wants to create. With the memo half finished, she then switches to signing payroll checks that are due that day. Jane's desk (and her living room, too) is stacked with magazines and books that she will read for a few minutes and then put down. She always plans to go back and finish them later. At home, though, Jane loves to garden. She can work on planting, potting, even weeding, for hours at a time. At those times, she feels totally absorbed in her work. She finishes feeling tired but strangely relaxed.

Attentional problems in ADD are primarily problems with regulating attention. Calling attention into action when needed and then maintaining it is the problem. ADDers notice things. They have difficulty screening out distractions, such as a conversation next door or the hum of the air conditioner; they are highly susceptible to distractions and can have difficulty controlling attention when needed.

Impulsivity

The inability to put on the brakes—or even find them—is the second defining characteristic of ADD. A person with ADD can find it difficult to inhibit thoughts, speech, and action. The person with ADD often blurts out an answer before the question is asked or says exactly what's on his mind at the moment, regardless of the consequences. The ADDer is usually the one at the party apologizing to the host—saying, "I'm so sorry. I really didn't mean to say that." It's also difficult for the ADDer to stop an action before it starts.

> John doesn't just have problems saying the wrong things at the wrong time. He has difficulty controlling his urge to gamble. He likes the thrill of not knowing what's going to happen next; the excitement of possibly winning big. Over time, though, gambling has caused problems. John is in debt. He borrows from credit cards to cover expenses and took out a second mortgage to consolidate bills to keep from losing everything. John drinks to forget his problems and to calm his nerves. Before he realizes it, he's sitting in front of the TV with a beer in hand. He reaches for alcohol without thinking. His wife complains and throws out liquor bottles when he is not looking. This enrages him, and he loses his temper with her. John has a general problem with impulse control; unfortunately, his

technique for coping with this problem also involves impulsivity, and
drinking, which in turn makes controlling the impulse of anger more difficult.

Without thinking, the person with ADD may take off to ski in the mountains—even when a major deadline looms near. Impulsive behavior may take more subtle forms, too, such as just rushing through an assignment without checking for errors. A little impulsivity is a good thing; we need spontaneity in our lives. But in ADD the ability to catch the impulse and make a reasoned decision to act can be an enormously difficult task.

Hyperactivity

For years hyperactivity was synonymous with ADD. Hyperkinetic children bouncing off walls was the research and clinical focus of ADD. Hyperactivity in adults, though, can be more subtle. Some ADD adults are on the go, go, go; others are quiet and may even appear calm. ADD adults often seem restless. The ADDer may jingle keys or tap a foot while trying to listen to others. Hyperactivity in adults also may take the form of excessive talking or an especially rapid rate of speech. Like attention, hyperactivity is primarily a problem of regulation. The ADDer finds it difficult to speed up or slow down thoughts, speech, and actions as needed.

Years ago, Herman skied, drove stock cars, and even taught ballroom dancing. Today in his professional life, as director of a psychology department at a Midwestern university, his hyperactivity causes him some problems. Heading department meetings is torture. He drums the table with his pencil, crosses and uncrosses his legs. He can't sit still, so he is up out of his chair walking around the room as he thinks through topics of discussion. His thoughts race, and he never hears anyone out. He interrupts midsentence with a related idea. He talks as fast as he thinks. Herman is constantly running—in marathons for recreation—and at the university, too. Walking around campus with him is an exhausting experience for most people. At parties he is like a bull in a china shop. He bumps into people, spills drinks, and trips over the furniture. He frequently cuts himself shaving, and his wife hates sitting next to him in their small car, as she has taken more than one elbow as he turns and twists abruptly.

Like impulsivity, some hyperactivity can be a good thing: when the energy is directed to a task—focused—it can move mountains. In ADD, hyperactivity is typically the purposeless expenditure of energy. But with treatment, it can be harnessed.

While the big three—inattention, impulsivity, and hyperactivity—are the defining characteristics of ADD, a description of them alone does not capture the experience of having ADD. ADD is a feeling that things are happening all around you and you can't control them. Having ADD is a persistent sense of being out of sync with the world. As a result, you are constantly looking around to see what is happening and guessing about what you are supposed to do. This creates an external focus. Rather than looking inside for direction, the outside world is calling the shots. It's very difficult to develop self-confidence, composure, and identity under these circumstances. People with ADD are often called immature or selfish. It's understandable when you realize that the person with ADD experiences events quickly and as controlled by others.

Having ADD also involves a unique experience with time. For people with ADD, time has an elastic nature. It stretches into interminable intervals or scrunches up into power-packed little moments. People with ADD have a sense of urgency about time. Everything is important right now. It's then difficult to set priorities and to approach one task at a time. The result is often disorganization and incomplete work.

Diagnosis of ADD

Diagnosis of ADD in adults is increasing. From its almost unknown existence twenty years go, ADD is suspected to affect 2 to 22 percent of adults. Some clinicians feel that ADD is wildly overdiagnosed, and others feel that even at the upper end of the range, 22 percent, it is underdiagnosed. Why such controversy?

The problem is in accurately diagnosing ADD. At present there is no definitive test for its existence. Types of brain scans have been used for research purposes of comparing one group of people to another, but they are not useful for the clinical diagnosis of an individual. The recent explosion of interest in ADD has resulted in availability of self-tests, questionnaires, rating scales, and many good books on the topic. But ADD can only be diagnosed by a clinician trained and experienced in the area of ADD with adults. In-depth interviews covering childhood history and current work and social relationships are necessary. Only after such lengthy interviews can the diagnosis be made.

There are three types of ADD: (1) ADD with inattentiveness as the primary symptom; (2) ADD with impulsivity and hyperactivity as the major concerns; or (3) ADD with problems in both areas. It is important to note that problems of inattention, hyperactivity, and/or impulsivity must create a problem in daily life and that problems must exist in at least two settings. These criteria avoid overdiagnosing the person who functions quite well at home but has problems at work, for example, not because of ADD but due to the increased stress level. The problems associated with ADD also must be severe and pervasive.

Problems of inattentiveness, hyperactivity, and impulsivity must not be caused by any other condition. A qualified professional is required to rule out other conditions that may produce symptoms resembling ADD, such as some allergies or hypothyroidism. Other psychological conditions may look like ADD, too. Bipolar disorder (previously called manic-depression), anxiety, post-traumatic stress disorder, and others, result in symptoms of restlessness, poor concentration, and mood swings that look like ADD. Only a professional with extensive experience in ADD and other disorders can make this distinction. If you feel you need further clarification of your diagnosis, contact your primary care physician for referral to a specialist who can accurately diagnose and treat your symptoms.

ADD All Around Us

There may be something particularly American about ADD. We know that ADD is more frequently diagnosed in the United States than in England or Europe. This higher incidence may reflect our current awareness of ADD, or it may be a real phenomenon. The type of person who would choose to immigrate to a foreign land to find a better life fits well with the ADD profile. The high risk involved in leaving family and familiar surroundings is the kind of adventure that many restless ADD types would like.

Who Has ADD?

ADD is widespread in our population. It can be found in all socioeconomic classes, ages, and levels of intelligence. It is more frequently diagnosed in males. The ratio of male to female children with ADD is seven to one. Other studies report four to twelve times more male diagnoses than female.

There may be both biological and psychological reasons for the greater incidence among males. Females, in general, internalize frustration more than males. They are less likely to act out, and to have their symptoms recognized by others. Girls are also less likely to have hyperactivity accompanying ADD. In fact, females may exhibit a quiet kind of ADD. They may be lost in daydreams. As children, though, they were likely to have been quite active.

As a result, girls are typically diagnosed at a later age than boys. There are also biological hypotheses for the greater occurrence of ADD in males. Testosterone, a male hormone, is known to slow the development of the frontal lobes and the left hemisphere of the brain. Girls tend to have more mature frontal lobes and use them for more brain functions. Girls also have a better-developed *corpus callosum,* and the left and right hemispheres of the brain interconnect and communicate more than they do in boys. These brain-based differences may make the symptoms of ADD more manageable for girls than for boys.

ADD begins in childhood. There is no such thing as adult-onset ADD, although many adults in our hyperkinetic culture may feel that they must have come down with ADD. Symptoms of ADD may be evident by the age of 2. For children 6–12 diagnosed with ADD, 50 to 70 percent will carry the diagnosis into adolescence and 35 percent into late adolescence. The declining rate probably does not mean that ADD has gone away, but more likely that the problems of inattention are being managed and masked. Hyperactivity also diminishes with age. The restlessness of adult ADD may be less noticeable and less recognized.

Learning Disabilities and ADD

There is a correlation between learning disabilities, such as dyslexia and difficulty writing or reading, or problems with math, and ADD. Approximately 30 percent of adults with ADD will have learning disabilities. About 50 to 80 percent of children and adolescents with ADD have a learning disability. ADD can be treated with medication and behavioral interventions. Only environmental interventions—such as tutoring—can help with learning disabilities.

ADD in Degrees

ADD is not an all-or-nothing disorder. ADD occurs in degrees. It is possible to have a mild case that can be fairly easily managed. It is also possible to have severe symptoms that are almost incapacitating. Naturally, the fewer and milder the symptoms, the easier it will be to manage ADD. But even severe ADD can, with effort, medication, and support, be treated.

ADD is also inconsistent from day to day and place to place. It is possible to be highly distractible at work, but focus well in a library. Or, an ADDer may find it torture to sit through a lecture on microeconomics but tolerate a music concert well.

ADD is a complicated, varied disorder. It is difficult to diagnose. It is also difficult to live with. Fortunately, treatment is improving almost as fast as our knowledge of ADD.

The symptoms of ADD vary daily. On some days, attention may be regulated with minimal effort, and other days are much more difficult. Impulsivity and hyperactivity also vary in severity. We do not know what causes these day-to-day changes. Mood, sleep, stress, and other factors may play a role. The one consistent aspect of ADD will be its inconsistency.

How to Use This Book

This book is written for the adult diagnosed with ADD. Some aspects of diagnosis are reviewed, but there is no attempt to make a diagnosis. If you feel you have ADD but aren't sure, see a professional. Do not attempt diagnosis on your own. ADD is one of the trickiest diagnoses to get right, and only an experienced professional can do it. This book also does not cover medication except to respect and support its role in treatment. Medications have been tremendously helpful in relieving symptoms of ADD. Ritalin, the most prescribed medication, is 70 to 80 percent effective in calming the storm of hyperactivity, and impulsivity, and in improving attention. Although effective, medication does not help 20 to 30 percent of adults with ADD. Learning to cope with ADD-related problems, then, becomes an all-important focus.

This book is written to help you work through the most frequently encountered problems related to ADD. You can use this book on your own. It's written to be applied to practical, everyday problems you may encounter. This book also can be used by support groups, coaches, or as an adjunct to therapy. It is written as a workbook, and self-assessment questions and exercises accompany almost every section. It's very important that you take the time to answer the questions and try the exercises. Your efforts will give you insight on both problems and solutions. Only by bringing it home in a personal way can you learn the techniques and make your reading really pay off.

Feel free to skip around in the chapter order. The chapters are largely independent of each other and don't need to be read straight through. The chart on the next page lists the main problem areas and where they are covered in detail in the book. You may want to start with chapters that seem most important to you now. But go back and read the other chapters at a later time. You'll need them to eventually get the whole picture of what ADD is and how it affects you. And, reread chapters from time to time. Knowledge has many layers. Each time you reread a chapter, reassess your situation, and apply the techniques to new problems, you'll deepen and strengthen what you know. As a result, you'll be increasingly effective in what you've chosen to do.

Summary

- Some of the things we know about ADD are that it *is a neurological condition* that makes it more difficult to regulate attention and to control impulses; it can be inherited; and it *always* begins in childhood. ADD can be found in all socioeconomic

Problem Area	Chapter 4 Self-Esteem	Chapter 5 Rational Thinking	Chapter 6 Focusing	Chapter 7 Finishing	Chapter 8 Mood Management	Chapter 9 Impulsivity	Chapter 10 Learning Skills	Chapter 11 Social Skills
Attention			X	X			X	
Hyperactivity					X			X
Impulsivity					X	X		
Self-esteem	X	X						X
Depression	X	X						
Mood			X	X	X	X		
Substance abuse					X	X		
Memory			X	X			X	
Sleep					X			
Disorganization			X	X			X	
Anxiety		X			X		X	
Relationships and social problems					X			X

classes, ages, and levels of intelligence; but it is much more common in males than in females.

- ADD should *not* be self-diagnosed. Many symptoms resembling ADD may be produced by other conditions. An experienced clinician can correctly diagnose ADD by conducting in-depth interviews covering childhood history and current work patterns and social relationships.

- Although medication can be helpful, learning new ways to overcome ADD-related problems is the key part of treatment. The self-assessment questions and exercises in this book will help you understand how ADD affects you and give you insight on new techniques for dealing with the problems and using your ADD strengths to your advantage.

2

So You Have ADD:

Recognizing Your Strengths and Weaknesses

ADDers have many strengths and skills. Ed Hallowell and John Ratey, authors of *Driven to Distraction,* have significantly advanced our knowledge of the positive aspects of ADD. Published in 1993, the book became an immediate best-seller and brought the existence of ADD to the attention of millions of Americans. The authors went beyond a dry, academic description and presented ADD as people experience it. Rather than clinical subjects, ADDers are described as complete people, with strengths as well as weaknesses. ADD may be the first disorder not to be seen in only pathological terms. ADD is challenging, but not without inner resources, too. When the problems related to ADD are managed, the strengths associated with ADD can shine and be applied more successfully to your goals.

This chapter describes the traits—both positive and negative—that stand out in people with ADD. The brief question-and-answer exercises are intended to help you assess your ADD; to find out which elements make up your own personal style.

ADD Strengths

If you have heard the expression, "every strength is a man's weakness," then the opposite is true for ADD. Every ADD problem has a flip side—a strength—that can be used to cope with ADD and enhance life. Not everyone with ADD has all of the strengths associated with it. Each person is unique and may have some of the positives often associated with ADD to some degree.

Creativity

Creativity is often associated ADD. Studies of children with ADD support this common observation. People with ADD are often flexible thinkers. They tend not to think about things the way they "should" but let their minds cross ordinary boundaries and put things together in new ways. A person with ADD can be very effective in a brainstorming session. The ADDer is likely to come up with a number of novel ideas—some off the wall and some quite solid. Another form of original thinking is the ADDer's ability to think abstractly. A person with ADD can often detach from a situation, stand back, and see it like it really is. Many ADDers have the ability to sum things up in a clean, simple way. ADDers express their creativity in every possible way—music, dance, art, drama, cooking, lively conversations, new solutions to old problems, to name a few.

1. Can I think in some creative ways?

_____

2. What was a good idea I had recently?

_____

3. How do I express my creativity (for example, music, dance, art, drama, writing, cooking, gardening, sewing, computing, mechanics, carpentry, sports)?

_____

Sense of Humor

Closely related to creativity is the ADDer's sense of humor. Making a joke takes a flexible mind. Humor is often derived from seeing something as it is and casting it in a new light. Many comedians do this when they let us see our politicians—or ourselves—in a completely different light. Other humor may be more physical, such as the slapstick of the Three Stooges or Keystone Cops. Whatever the type of humor, a fresh twist is placed on some familiar topics.

Having a good sense of humor doesn't require making jokes. The ability to "get" and appreciate humor is important, too. Being able to laugh at a funny situation requires the same mental flexibility as creating humor. The ability to see things as they are and then turn them sideways or upside down is used. Humor is one of the great coping skills. You can take it anywhere, it requires no money, and results in tension reduction. Humor will be discussed again on the topic of mood management in chapter 8.

1. Do I have a pretty good sense of humor? Yes _____ No _____

2. Can I make others laugh? Yes _____ No _____

3. Do I laugh at the humor of others? Yes _____ No _____

4. Who are my favorite comedians? _____

   Favorite TV comedy? _____

   Favorite movie comedy? _____

   Favorite funny book? _____

Lack of Inhibition

Impulsivity is one of the three defining characteristics of ADD. In the wrong setting, impulsivity can cause problems, such as drinking and driving or buying without thinking. Impulsivity, or lack of inhibition, at the right time and place can lead to new opportunities—for example, striking up a conversation with a co-worker at lunch. Other times, impulsivity may result in trying a new book, restaurant, or activity, and finding a great new experience.

Whether spontaneity results in new relationships, business ventures, or any other endeavor, it can be gratifying to try. Spontaneity feels good. It can make you feel free—alive.

1. What risk have I taken lately? _____

2. Have I ever benefited from being spontaneous? _____

3. What risks would I like to take in the future? _____

_____

High-Level Energy

The hyperactivity of childhood ADD may continue into adulthood. It is somewhat more common for this overactivity to be toned down into physical restlessness, and it is possible to have a quiet, dreamy kind of ADD. But many adults with ADD need to move around. They are uncomfortable when confined to one place for a period of time—even for a few minutes in extreme cases. Adults with ADD tend to have more energy to burn than adults without ADD. This increased energy can be an advantage. When focused, this energy can move mountains. An ADDer whose mind is made up to get something done can work at it for hours with sustained energy. These whirlwinds of activity leave the non-ADD adult exhausted from watching.

You can channel the high energy of ADD to good purpose. Adults with ADD often become successful entrepreneurs. Starting a business takes long, long hours. The ADDer may have the creativity to design a new endeavor, and with enough energy to stay on the go for hours if not days, the ADDer can succeed in this high-risk phase of business.

1. Do others comment on my high energy level? Yes _____ No _____

2. Do I feel the need to be moving? Yes _____ No _____

3. What have I spent a lot of energy on lately? _____

4. Where would I like to focus my energy? _____

Ability to Hyperfocus

Although problems in mustering and maintaining attention are the hallmark of ADD, the ability to focus extremely well and for long periods of time characterizes ADD, too. This ability to focus intensely, called *hyperfocusing,* is a state when attention is so specifically focused that almost nothing else exists at that moment. Most people have had the experience of losing themselves in a book and not hearing someone call their name. For ADDers this ability to focus so specifically can occur frequently. Hyperfocusing occurs when there is intense interest in the subject.

A feeling of satisfaction often follows an experience of hyperfocusing. It is gratifying to lose yourself completely in an activity. Hyperfocusing is like what top athletes call "the zone."

1. Can I remember a time when I was so focused that I did not hear what was going on around me? Yes _____ No _____

2. On what tasks do I hyperfocus? Yes _____ No _____

3. How do I feel after an experience of hyperfocusing?

_____

This is a period of time when the ace runner, basketball player, or other athlete feels so much a part of the sport that everything else is suspended for that moment.

In addition to being a pleasurable experience and a real boon to getting things done, the ability to hyperfocus can be an essential aspect in some careers. ADDers who can hyperfocus make good crisis workers, such as emergency medical technicians or fire or police personnel. They seem to become calmer in the midst of chaos and can solve immediate problems well.

Willingness to Take Risks

An increased willingness to take risks is often found in adults with ADD. Taking reasonable risks can create results for some. Any new endeavor includes risk. A dream to start a business, new relationship, or return to school can be planned and researched, but then it's always necessary to leap into the unknown. The impatience that often accompanies ADD can lead some people to take the plunge—ADDers are more inclined to try, instead of sitting on the sidelines as opportunity and life pass by.

Risk taking is essential for some lines of work. ADDers with this asset have many occupations to consider: financial investor, stockbroker, explorer, scientist, artist. These and other occupations require certain risk taking because the result of the work is not certain—any outcome is possible.

1. What risks have I taken lately?

_____

2. Have I benefited from taking risks?

_____

3. What risks would I like to take in the future?

_____

Other Strengths

A number of clinicians note that ADDers seem to be able to see through a facade and to quickly and accurately assess the true motivation of others. Resourcefulness, tenacity, and loyalty are also noted in ADDers. And, people with ADD are often warmhearted and forgiving. ADDers with all of these traits can make good mental health professionals.

Problems Related to ADD

We began with the many positive attributes and assets directly related to ADD, but, of course, there are a number of problem areas accompanying the disorder. Problems with attention, hyperactivity, and impulsivity are the defining characteristics of ADD. But those who have ADD know it is much more. ADD affects all aspects of life, and by the time adulthood is reached, problems are compounded. Relationships, education, vocation, and personal fulfillment are affected.

Some problems may be related to the neurological basis of ADD—for example, impaired memory, sleep, and mood disturbances. Others, such as decreased self-esteem and depression are more likely a result of living and coping with ADD. Not everyone with ADD will have identified his or her problems. But if you do see some of the areas as pertaining to you, take note. You can then direct your reading to the areas where you most need help.

Low Self-Esteem

Impaired self-esteem is the most pervasive problem associated with ADD. Kevin Murphy, director of the ADD clinic at the University of Massachusetts, notes that 85 percent of his clients have difficulty in this area. ADDers often live with a sense of underachievement. They feel intense frustration regarding their inability to meet their potential. They see others complete simple day-to-day tasks without a monumental struggle and wonder, "What is wrong with me? Why can't I do that?" Constant frustration leads to self-doubt and a decreased feeling of worth. Other people often compound the problem. Throughout life you have doubtlessly heard, "Why can't you pay attention? Why can't you ever finish what you start? Why can't you get it?" These barrages are not exactly uplifting. In fact, repeated exposure to criticism, real or implied, hurts your sense of self-worth.

Do I feel that I haven't accomplished as much as I should?   Yes _____   No _____

Depression

Between 35 and 40 percent of clients at the University of Massachusetts clinic are being treated for depression. Kathleen Nadeau reports that major depression affects about 10 percent of ADDers, and 25 percent have a milder form called *dysthymia*. Depression appears in many forms. Some depressed people are low in energy and enthusiasm and feel that life is unrewarding or even not worth living. Others are increasingly restless and aggressive, but still feel down on life and express little hope for themselves.

Many factors in an ADDer's life can lead to depression. A person with ADD often suffers a sense of inferiority, resulting from repeated effort and failure. These experiences typically begin early in life. Problems managing impulses in playing with other children and issues about performance in school often begin what becomes a lifelong struggle to make it in the world. ADDers try to hide their difficulties in coping with daily life and to cover up their past failures. As a result they feel like impostors. This sense of needing to hide your true self is confusing, frustrating, and depressing.

Depression is often the issue that brings the ADDer to the therapist's office. Poor concentration, disorganization, sleep disturbance, and restlessness may be attributed to depression when the problem really is ADD. It takes a skilled clinician to tell the difference.

Depression is a problem that I would like to work on. Yes _____ No _____

Moodiness

The moods of an adult with ADD are like a ride on a roller coaster. Swings from excited highs to down-and-out lows are common. People with ADD are often thin-skinned. An unexpected criticism can ruin an otherwise fine day. ADDers tend to concentrate on losses. They wonder over and over how events turned out so badly and what they could have done differently. ADDers have difficulty regulating their responses to situations. They can become exuberant over minor triumphs and outraged over seemingly small slights from others.

Because ADDers can be intense and respond strongly to their surroundings, they are exciting to be around. But the excitement wears thin after a while. Friends and family want periods of calm and stability. Those involved with an ADDer are often confused and exhausted by the unpredictable mood swings, and relationship problems are a common fallout of these ongoing conflicts.

Do I experience highs and lows that I can't control? Yes _____ No _____

Substance Abuse

Many ADDers tend to abuse various substances. Kevin Murphy estimates that 35 percent of adults seen in the University of Massachusetts clinic are abusing substances. The drugs of choice are alcohol and marijuana. Adolescent ADDers may start using substances as a way of fitting in with peers. People with ADD don't make friends easily, and sometimes drugs and alcohol can create a bond that is otherwise hard to find. Adults with ADD typically abuse substances as a form of self-medication. Drinking, smoking, and the like, help dull the pain of troubled careers and relationships and temporarily relieve the internal beating ADDers give themselves for perceived failures.

Substance abuse provides very temporary relief. After sobering up, the original problem is, of course, still there. Substance abuse in the long run makes things worse. Alcohol, in particular, further diminishes your ability to concentrate, and it dulls memory. Substance abuse also increases impulsivity and, especially, the propensity to violence. It affects relationships with others and further compounds the ADDer's difficulty in maintaining a marriage and career.

Do I use alcohol or drugs as a means of feeling better or fitting in with others?
Yes _____ No _____

Memory Problems

Problems with memory are called the "silent symptom" of ADD. Forgetfulness just doesn't draw the attention that hyperactivity or even impulsivity does. But poor memory is directly linked to ADD through the problems of inattentiveness and distractibility. After all, to remember something requires that you first attend to it.

Memory is often thought to be "good" or "bad," but there are several types of memory and you may not have problems in all areas. ADDers do frequently have problems remembering a string of verbal directions or other verbal information, such as dates, names, or facts. They also have problems remembering what they are supposed to do. The experience of walking into a room and forgetting why you went there is a common one, but for ADDers, it may happen frequently—even several times a day.

Do I often have trouble remembering directions, names, dates, facts, or what I'm supposed to do? Yes _____ No _____

Sleep Disturbances

A good night's sleep is critical for daytime alertness and stable moods. But sleep disturbances frequently accompany ADD. People with ADD often report that just as everyone else is settling down to sleep, they become energized and want to be active. They may stay up late frequently and as a result get too little sleep to be rested the following day. ADDers also report difficulty falling asleep due to racing thoughts. Their minds are going at full speed—reviewing the events of the day, ruminating over problems and their reactions, and thinking of what to do tomorrow. Still others report problems awakening throughout the night. Some ADDers wake up as often as five or six times each night.

Whether the problem is difficulty falling asleep or staying asleep, the result is the same—decreased daytime alertness. ADDers often feel drowsy during the day and have an even harder time paying attention. Decreased sleep also is known to affect mood adversely. Increased irritability and loss of control may result.

Do I have frequent trouble falling or staying asleep at night?   Yes _____   No _____

Disorganization

Difficulty getting organized is a common complaint among ADDers. Adults with ADD often have problems with work that must be completed by following a sequence of steps. ADDers are impatient and tend to jump ahead, trying to skip a few steps especially if they aren't interested. The result is a poorly finished task. As a result of distractions and poor memory, ADDers often forget where they are in a task. Filing, for example, is difficult for people with ADD. They tend to have several different filing systems at one time.

ADDers are also overaroused. They become overwhelmed easily by a task, thinking that it requires so much time and effort that they just can't do it. Other times they feel so overwhelmed that they don't know where to start. They tend to shut down as a result and not get started. Procrastination is a big problem for ADDers, whether it is on small jobs such as cleaning the closet or major life events such as going back to school. Adults with ADD report a lot of anxiety and tension as a result of their procrastination.

Do I have difficulty getting or staying organized in my personal or professional life?
Yes _____   No _____

Do I often procrastinate?   Yes _____   No _____

Anxiety

ADDers have an overaroused nervous system. When they are startled, they have a strong response, and it takes them longer than other people to return to a calm state. It may be this tendency to startle easily that is related to increased anxiety for some ADDers. About 30 percent of adults with ADD have an anxiety disorder. Some evidence indicates that ADDers without hyperactivity are more prone to anxiety. Changes in plans or any unexpected transition can cause the ADDer anxiety. During these times the person with ADD feels on alert—hypervigilant—for danger. Chronic stress for the ADDer can result in an anxiety disorder.

Anxiety for ADDers also results from environmental experience. A person with ADD may have experienced failure in a situation and, when placed in the same situation, begins to feel anxious. Whenever fear of failure exists, people tend to avoid the situation. Avoidance, unfortunately, lets the fear fester and grow since no experience is allowed that challenges it. ADDers are also prone to social phobias. A history of saying the wrong thing, blurting out some opinion, or being punished for interrupting or for physical restlessness, lead some adult ADDers to feel anxious and to avoid others.

Do I get anxious often?   Yes _____   No _____

Difficulties in Relationships and Social Situations

ADDers are impatient. They find it difficult to wait in line, fill out forms, and perform other small, everyday tasks. They also find it difficult to pay attention to what others are saying and to tolerate emotions. As a result, those involved with an ADD adult often feel ignored, taken for granted, or snubbed. The ADDer wants to terminate the conversation and move on. When social events occur, they are inclined to "just get it over with." ADDers are easily bored and constantly looking for the next source of stimulation. An ADDer finds it difficult to focus on one person long enough to get to know that person and understand him or her. And, the person with ADD is known to have mood swings and intense reactions that can be difficult for a loved one to accept. Problems in intimate relationships are common, and adult ADDers have higher rates of divorce and separation than non-ADD adults.

ADDers have difficulty in less intimate social relationships, too. About 75 percent of ADDers grow up to have problems in the social areas of their lives. Impulsivity often leads the person with ADD to blurt out thoughts or opinions before thinking. ADDers often interrupt others, possibly because they are afraid if they don't say it now, they'll forget. As a result, ADDers often are thought to be rude and overbearing.

Do I have difficulty making and maintaining relationships with others?
Yes _____   No _____

ADD Styles

Many efforts have been made to characterize the "ADD personality." ADDers are described as the absentminded professor, or the dumb blonde, or just as outgoing types. Some ADDers may fit these profiles, but there is no definitive ADD personality. ADDers are as varied in who they are as anyone. ADDers do, however, develop a few common styles to cope with their symptoms. These styles grow over years. By the time adulthood is reached, the styles are pretty well developed and may seem permanent. Although we describe distinct profiles here, in real life, pure types rarely exist. You may find that you fit one or more of the profiles. One coping style may predominate, but you may employ others, depending on the situation or your mood.

Let's Party

The first coping style is essentially a way of not coping. Some ADDers have tried and failed so many times to get organized, manage anger, or make friends, that they give up.

> Fred copes by not trying anymore. He distracts himself with alcohol, friends, and music. He is 25 and had a very difficult time in school. His outbursts got him into trouble with teachers and peers. His grades were poor and he passed from grade to grade without really learning a lot. He is very bright, and the frustration of not doing as well as he feels he can creates tension and depression for him. Fred drives a cab during the day. His driving is aggressive, and he spends most nights at the local bar or rock club. Fred and his friends drink a lot. On weekends the blowouts last all day and night. He has energy and humor and is a lot of fun to be with, at least until he passes out. Fred rarely recovers long enough to reflect on his behavior. He doesn't really care. Nothing else worked for him, so why not just have fun? At least he's good at it.

Others may use shopping or gambling to numb the pain of failure. In the long run the money and health run out, and you are left to face the reality of life.

Poor Me

The "poor me" approach to coping with ADD leaves the adult feeling overburdened and depressed. The adult feels alone, helpless, and angry about the constant frustration of daily life.

1. Do I distract myself with drugs, alcohol, shopping, for example? Yes _____ No _____

2. Which "substance" do I use most? _____

3. Does my social life revolve around this activity? Yes _____ No _____

4. Do I have other activities that I enjoy and that occupy my time? Yes _____ No _____

Tom is angry. He feels the world is a treacherous place and there isn't much that can be done about it. He has a quick temper, and his defenses are easily triggered. Tom feels that he's gotten a raw deal. He looks at others who have succeeded in ways he can't and envies them. He's frustrated that others do easily what takes him hours and days to complete. He reacts to his ADD by blaming others. Tom blames his parents for not being supportive, his teachers for being insensitive, and employers for not caring or helping. When his relationships with women break down, he blames them for being too demanding and selfish. Tom slaves away at a job less than his ability deserves. He has little chance at present to pull himself out of his situation. His sarcasm seeps out at all the wrong times. His boss is aware of his hotheadedness and is reluctant to promote him.

1. Do I feel I have gotten a raw deal in life? Yes _____ No _____

2. Do I feel others have let me down? They have not understood, cared, or been as patient as they could? Yes _____ No _____

3. Do I feel that the world is a treacherous place? Yes _____ No _____

4. Do I feel that my future won't be much different than my past? Yes _____ No _____

It's My Way

Some adults take a very active approach to managing ADD. Rather than giving up or sulking, they jump right in and take control. Control then becomes their way of coping with anxiety, frustration, and loss.

Arlene takes control of every situation she can. From the moment you enter her office, she is "on." She is alert and trying hard to concentrate. She asks all the questions. It's hard to get your agenda on the table at all. Arlene has found that when she leads the conversation, she is less petrified of missing information and appearing stupid. Arlene carries her drive for control over to her personal life. She must decide when and where friends meet. She dominates the conversation there, too. Her friends love her energy, wit, and varied interests, but they cringe with frustration as she always must have the last word, and of course, she's right about everything. Arlene is aware of her control issue but feels justified since she needs to manage a severe disorder that leaves her with a sense of chaos all around her.

Attempting to take control of your life is a healthy act. But not knowing when to let go creates problems on top of the ADD symptoms that control is intended to manage.

1. Do I often control people, conversations, events in my life? Yes _____ No _____

2. Do I always get the last word? Yes _____ No _____

3. Do others tell me I need to "lighten up?" Yes _____ No _____

4. Do I have trouble letting others make decisions or be right? Yes _____ No _____

Out of My Way

Like the controller, the aggressor dominates in an attempt to control the feelings of chaos. But aggressors tend to have more anger behind their actions. The aggressor is impatient and can't wait long enough to hear anyone out or deal with feelings. So the aggressor just mows them down.

Sean works as an accounts manager with a software firm. He's successful at his work since it involves extensive use of the computer and he can focus on the bottom line. He's deferential to superiors, but with his staff he's known as a tyrant. He wants everything done yesterday. He makes sarcastic remarks to employees when their work is slower than he prefers. He never stops to say thanks or to commend a good job. He's on to the next task. Unfortunately, his department is regarded as highly efficient, and he has no motivation to change. Sean is less successful in his personal life. His family feels as if they're living with a drill sergeant. He's often not sensitive to his wife's headaches, and he seems oblivious to his children's feelings of powerlessness.

1. Am I often impatient with the feelings or behavior of others? Yes _____ No _____

2. Do others tell me I'm insensitive? Yes _____ No _____

3. Do I feel justified in overlooking my impact on others because they're just complainers? Yes _____ No _____

4. Can I see that my family is often angry or afraid of me? Yes _____ No _____

Help Me

People with ADD often feel overwhelmed. They tend to see the big picture. When looking at a project in its entirety, it's easy to see how the feeling of being overwhelmed occurs.

Some ADDers are aware of this feeling, but they don't know what to do about it. Some reach out to others since they feel they just can't manage by themselves.

> Charles is a great-looking guy, very athletic, and personable. He never had any trouble attracting female attention. Even in elementary school, girls would let him copy their homework. He got through school with a lot of help from teachers and classmates. In the work world, Charles looks to co-workers for help. He often pawns his work off on females who are anxious to please him. He ducks responsibility at every turn. Charles feels just fine about his coping strategy. He feels that he is somehow entitled to the service he receives—mainly from females. He does not make any effort to reciprocate when his helpers are in distress. Charles's strategy will work well as long as his looks and charm hold out and there are plenty of people willing to help him.

1. Do others seem willing to help me out when I need it? Yes _____ No _____

2. Do I just expect that there will be others around to get the work done when I need it? Yes _____ No _____

3. Do I help others when they are in a tough spot? Yes _____ No _____

I Need My Space

Finally, some ADDers cope by eliminating as much stress from life as possible. The result of this strategy is a fairly restricted lifestyle, but it does serve the purpose of reducing those feelings of being overwhelmed and the possibility of failure.

> Peggy has a quiet, daydream-like type of ADD. She is imaginative and, as a child, entertained herself for hours by making up fantastic stories of adventure and romance. She drifted through school and had only one or two close friends. She was very anxious around men and avoided dating. When Peggy left the protective confines of her parents' home, she was hardly prepared for the bombardment of adult life. She tried living with roommates but couldn't stand the pressure to be social. She moved to a studio apartment and has lived alone for years. She goes directly home from work on most nights. Her apartment is very neat. She can't stand the stimulation of anything being out of place. She doesn't subscribe to magazines because she can't stand the pressure to keep up with the reading. Peggy needs a quiet, highly organized environment. She requires one or two hours each night of just sitting and letting her mind clear out of all the stimulation of the day. Peggy particularly avoids men. Meeting a

man she likes puts her general level of anxiety into overdrive. She can be so rattled after a date that she loses an entire night of sleep. It just feels better to Peggy to lead a quiet, simple life that she can manage.

1. Do I dread social events, fearing that I'll be uncomfortable?   Yes _____   No _____

2. Do I require a good deal of time each day just to let my thoughts clear out?
   Yes _____   No _____

3. Do I need to control the amount of stimulation I encounter each day?   Yes _____
   No _____

4. Do I avoid friends or dates that make me feel overstimulated and out of control?
   Yes _____   No _____

Stages of Acceptance

When first diagnosed, it's common for ADDers to feel relief. You feel better when something you have been struggling with is recognized as a valid medical condition. Giving it a name brings it into focus. You're not alone—a lot of others have been struggling to manage the same problems of restlessness, impulsivity, and inattention. ADDers typically describe a major sense of relief that it is close to euphoria after diagnosis. Following this initial period, you will again feel and respond to the problems ADD creates for you in your life. You will begin to move through the stages of acceptance.

Elizabeth Kubler-Ross has described five stages of acceptance: denial, anger, bargaining, depression, and acceptance. The stages were initially identified as a process of accepting death but have been extended to any process of accepting loss. After the initial positive experience of finally being diagnosed, typically, an adult will begin to look back over life through the ADD lens. You will identify lot of losses and regrets. It's natural to experience some sadness over lost opportunities.

It's important to work through the stages of acceptance. In doing so you'll be in a good position to make the changes that will enable you to reach your potential by putting your ADD strengths to work. Carefully consider the stages outlined here, and identify where you are in your acceptance process.

Stage One: Denial

Denial may not seem like a stage of acceptance. In this stage you are minimizing the impact that ADD has for you and your future. You may even question the diagnosis itself. Some people take up the opposition and feel that there is no such thing as ADD—it's just an excuse. More often though, the ADDer in denial will downplay the diagnosis, saying, "Well, I think my case is a mild one." Others say, "So what if I have ADD? It's not going to be a problem for me." Denial is an understandable response to diagnosis. You want to get on with life and not be slowed down dealing with another problem. Unfortunately, it rarely works this way. Few people who are diagnosed with ADD have a minor problem with it. Coming to terms with your diagnosis and realizing that it means change is the first step in acceptance.

1. Do I feel that ADD doesn't require that I make changes in how I live? Yes _____ No _____

2. Do I feel that I can really get along without prescription medication? Yes _____ No _____

3. Do I sometimes wonder if ADD is really just an excuse? Yes _____ No _____

4. Do I feel that my ADD is not serious—that I can just handle it? Yes _____ No _____

Stage Two: Anger

Denial usually collides with reality at some point. Typically an event occurs that makes you aware of ADD and its impact. This event may be loss of a job, dissolution of a marriage, or financial loss. The loss can be linked to ADD. At this point, frustration and anger build. The ADDer may direct anger toward the diagnosis and say, "Why? Why me? Why do I have to deal with this?" Anger may be directed outward to others who don't have ADD and whose lives are perceived to be so much easier. Finally, anger may be directed at yourself. Some ADDers heap criticism on themselves, call themselves names, and generally berate their character. Anger is a difficult emotion to handle well, and it puts the ADDer at risk for further problems.

1. Have I had a recent loss or disappointment that can be linked to ADD? Yes _____ No _____

2. Do I feel resentful that I have to have ADD? Yes _____ No _____

3. Do I look at others who don't have ADD and feel envy or resentment? Yes _____ No _____

4. Do I feel mad a lot of the time? Yes _____ No _____

Stage Three: Bargaining

When anger simmers down, you are next likely to take a rational approach to dealing with ADD. You begin to make deals with ADD. Most often this stage involves striking a bargain concerning medication. You feel that if you take medication as prescribed, problems should be gone. You may feel that you'll go to support group meetings or therapy, and that's your end of the deal. The ADD should respond and not be a problem anymore.

Bargaining is an active step toward ADD management. But it falls short because it's an all-or-nothing kind of thinking. If you do all of your part, then ADD should not be a problem anymore. Problems, of course, don't go away, and this will lead you to stage four.

1. Am I looking for some ways to make ADD not a problem for me? Yes _____ No _____

2. Do I feel that I'm doing my part to manage ADD? Yes _____ No _____

3. Do I feel that if I do "all the right things" that ADD won't be a problem for me?
Yes _____ No _____

Stage Four: Depression

Bargains fail. ADD continues to be a problem. It's frustrating and discouraging to someone who followed the plan to manage ADD. With great effort, a medication schedule may have been tried, therapy appointments kept, but problems still occur. In all fairness, these may be new problems—ones that the previous bargain could not cover; but you still feel let down. Often ADDers feel tired at this point and wish they could go back to the way things were before ADD was diagnosed. Trying to deal with ADD has taken a lot of time, effort, and energy, and it's still there!

Depression is a common and serious problem for people with ADD. It can be especially tough if you don't have an adequate support group. You can wind up feeling alone. As tough as this stage is, it's necessary to not stop here. With some more effort, support, and a plan, you can feel the loss and get through it to greater understanding and self-acceptance.

1. Am I tired of trying to manage ADD? Yes _____ No _____

2. Do I sometimes feel very alone with ADD? Yes _____ No _____

3. Do I wish I could go back to before I knew I had ADD? Yes _____ No _____

Stage Five: Acceptance

After all the false starts and disappointments of previous stages, acceptance brings a kind of peace. You've used up a lot of your will to struggle and are now in a calmer, more rational state. At this point you have the greatest chance of looking ADD in the eye and accepting it as a permanent part of your life. You are likely to spend less time hiding your faults. You're less apologetic and have a decreased need to attack others out of self-protection. You may begin to feel hopeful about life and your ability to learn to live with ADD.

1. Have I been less careful to hide myself and problems lately? Yes _____ No _____

2. Do I feel less angry or threatened about having ADD? Yes _____ No _____

3. Do I feel that I can live with ADD? Yes _____ No _____

4. Do I feel that I can continue to learn, accept, and manage ADD? Yes _____ No _____

It's not likely that you'll progress straight through the stages of acceptance on one try. More often, ADDers get stuck in one stage for a long time. It's also possible to slip back to previous stages from time to time. You'll then pick up the process again and move forward through the stages. Eventually, and usually with support from others, you can make it to acceptance and be in a position to put your ADD strengths to work to get the most out of your life.

Summary

- Many positive attributes are associated with ADD. Some identified strengths include humor, lack of inhibition, energy, and the ability to hyperfocus and take risks. ADDers are individuals. They may have some or all of these strengths in varying ways.

- The problems associated with ADD affect all aspects of life. ADDers may suffer from poor self-esteem, depression, mood swings, substance abuse, problems with memory, sleep disturbances, disorganization, anxiety, and problems in social relationships.

- There is no single ADD personality. Some styles of coping with ADD have been identified. Some ADDers manage by giving up the struggle with ADD and focusing on having fun. The "poor me" style blames others for the difficulty of ADD. The controller and the aggressor make every effort to dominate ADD and the people in their lives. The aggressor is angrier than the controller. Some ADDers cope by getting others to take care of them and their problems. Others cope by withdrawing from life and problems.

- Accepting ADD is a process that takes place in five stages. Denial that ADD is a problem occurs first. It is followed by a stage of anger when real problems are encountered. Bargaining comes next, when rigid rules are established. When the bargaining fails, depression occurs. In the final stage of acceptance, the struggle with ADD is no longer hidden or denied and forgiveness of self and others occurs.

3

Getting Started:

Commit to Change

Understanding and managing your ADD requires change on your part. As you learn about ADD, you see more of your behavior in understandable terms. Initially, you feel relief that your actions make sense. Following this relief, you start to face many of the habits and defenses you have developed to protect yourself from misunderstandings in the larger world. You begin the change process simply by recognizing that change is necessary and by wanting to change.

Six Stages of Change

James Prochaska, John Norcross, and Carlo DiClemente conducted extensive research on the change process and have identified six stages. The stages are reliable and occur in the same order for any kind of change:

1. Precontemplation—you avoid change and deny problems.

2. Contemplation—you accept the need to change and seek information.

3. Preparation—you make plans.

4. Action—you implement the plan.

5. Maintenance—you solidify your success.

6. Termination—you are comfortable with new behaviors, and your efforts to change can stop.

Identifying your stage of change is crucial for your success. It's also important to know that you may be in different stages for different problems. As an adult with ADD, you have had to cope with difficult circumstances for a long time. It's likely that you have developed more than one problematic behavior to defend yourself against criticism from others. You may be in the precontemplation stage for problem drinking or in the preparation stage for financial planning. The change experts agree that, while difficult, you can plan and act to change more than one behavior at a time.

Common to all stages of change is the need for support from others. Change is difficult and sometimes painful. Having supportive relationships will make a world of difference as you undertake this challenging process.

Precontemplation

To some, precontemplation is not a stage of change at all. For in the precontemplation stage, you resist change. You make every effort to avoid confronting the problem or dealing with it. This resistance usually takes the form of denying that you have a problem.

Ruben is in his late 40s and has worked for over twenty years as a salesman for the telephone company. His ADD was never diagnosed. He is away from home a lot and finds himself lonely and bored. He's restless after work. He began to erase the pain of long, hard days on the road by relaxing in a bar. Over the years his habit continued, and he is drinking three drinks a night during the week and a six-pack a night on weekends. His wife has noticed the increase in weekend drinking, and that Ruben sometimes slurs his speech in phone calls home. She mentioned her concerns to him, but he brushed them off. He accused her of wanting to live with a saint. He felt she had no basis for judging the amount of alcohol he drinks or can handle.

Ruben's response is typical. Alcoholism is called the "disease of denial." Like other precontemplators, Ruben sees no problem. When evidence is put before him, he easily dismisses it as someone else's concern. Because people in the precontemplation stage are in denial about a problem, they are terribly uninformed about the dangers their behavior can create. Precontemplators are often demoralized about their situation. Ruben is aware that he feels bad a great deal of the time. He just doesn't know why or what to do about it. Rather than change, Ruben continues to protect himself with maladaptive defenses. He blames his wife for not understanding his stress. He rationalizes his drinking, saying that he can handle his alcohol.

As an adult coping with ADD, you have undoubtedly encountered many difficult situations and been angry or frustrated about the expectations of others. Although you are reading this book and actively seeking information about ADD and its management, you may recognize some problems areas in which you are still in the precontemplative stage of change.

Contemplation

Contemplation is the stage when change begins. In this stage, you overcome denial and develop a desire for action. Unlike precontemplation, people in this stage actively seek information about the problem. They want to stop being stuck and to get on with the change

1. Have others suggested that I have a problem behavior to change? Yes _____ No _____

   If yes, what problems were identified for me? _____

2. Do I avoid information about problems others suggest I may have? Yes _____ No _____

3. Am I ever defensive when others mention a habit of mine? Yes _____ No _____

   If yes, describe such an instance. _____
   _____

process. At the same time, they are resolving ambivalence about changing. While change seems desirable, the fear of failure is uncomfortable.

> William is just emerging from his teens. Like other adolescents with ADD, he found school difficult. He was restless and dreaded sitting through class. He preferred to be out with his friends, riding bikes, skateboards, talking and smoking. William is thinking about becoming a police officer and feels he should quit smoking in order to pass the physical exam. William thinks about getting the nicotine patch, reads up on it, and may even join a smoking cessation group. He talks to others who have quit. Part of him hates to give up a comfortable old habit, and part of him wonders if he can. He thinks he'll get started—seriously—in about six months, sometime after the holidays, when life is a little bit less hectic.

William has passed the precontemplation stage. He does not deny that cigarettes are a problem. He doesn't reject information on smoking. In fact, he seeks it out. Like others in the contemplation stage, he's ambivalent. He likes his old habit and regrets giving it up. At other times, he's looking to the future and focusing on the benefits of change. At present, though, he is waiting. Six months is the typical time frame for those in the contemplation stage to plan to get started on their change program. His decision to wait gives him more time to savor the old ways and to discover the "perfect" time to act.

Preparation

In the preparation stage, plans for action move from the six-month time frame to within the next few months. Some ambivalence remains, but a decision has been made to move ahead with change. Commitment is the hallmark of the preparation stage. During this time you begin to focus on what needs to be done, when, how, and so on. Your thinking becomes focused, and you begin to set dates to begin and organize your work and to prioritize other responsibilities.

1. Do I actively seek information pertaining to problem behaviors I want to change?
   Yes _____ No _____

2. Do I plan to get started on my change efforts sometime in the next six months?
   Yes _____ No _____

3. Do I still feel some ambivalence about change? Yes _____ No _____

4. Do I worry sometimes if I can succeed? Yes _____ No _____

Sue has a long history of impulsive behavior. She was hyperactive as a child. In addition to being constantly in motion, she also had a quick temper. She picked fights with other kids and talked back to her parents and teachers. She was in trouble a lot and felt frustrated and defeated. Sue has finally reached the preparation stage in her lifelong battle with anger. She denied it for years until her husband threatened divorce and meant it. Sue quickly found reality and began thinking about her need for change. The urgency of the problem helped to resolve her ambivalence about giving up comfortable, old behavior.

In the preparation stage, Sue asked her husband for a time they could meet and talk things over quietly and calmly. At that time he made a statement of her commitment to change. Together, they began to set up a time each day to talk about problems before they reached the crisis stage. They agreed on a signal to warn each other about bad moods and discussed what they each wanted for support.

The preparation stage may be the most important stage for successful change. Change is difficult, and if it is not planned for carefully, progress can be derailed. It's important in the preparation stage to think of the problems that lie ahead. When will it be most difficult to persist with the planned change? What will you do if you slip? How will you respond to others' comments on your new behavior? Prochaska and colleagues report that half of American adults plan to change some behavior at the beginning of each new year. Seventy-seven percent succeed for one week, 55 percent for one month, 40 percent for six months, and only 19 percent remain successful after two years. They attribute most relapses to poor planning in the preparation stage of change.

1. Do I plan to make changes within the next four months? Yes _____ No _____

2. Am I beginning to be specific in thinking about how I could change? Yes _____
   No _____

3. Am I thinking more about the pros of changing than the cons? Yes _____ No _____

Action

The action stage is the most visible stage of change. In this stage you are implementing plans made during the previous stage—preparation.

Instead of acting out, Joyce became withdrawn as a result of ADD. Over the years she became increasingly depressed. She often relieved her darker mood by shopping. Spending money made her feel powerful and in control. Joyce broke through the denial of her impulsive shopping habit when she got into deep debt with her credit card companies. She prepared well for her change and worked out a repayment plan. She is now ready to implement her ideas and began by cutting up all of her credit cards, recording each of her cash expenditures in a daily log, and joining a group to keep herself busy and reduce the stress that usually leads to shopping. She has prepared well and is ready for the comments of her "friends" who love to go on shopping sprees with her. Joyce finds it most difficult to control her urges after visits home with her parents, but she is planning for this problem, too. She avoids unnecessary trips to their home, but when visits are necessary, she has a recovery plan. She goes to the library and browses for books to read. Joyce also finds support from some new friends who praise and congratulate her when she withstands the temptation to shop.

The action stage is the most exciting stage of change. You are finally doing something. There is a lot of hope at this point. It can also be anxiety provoking. People notice your change and comment on it. This attention may be stressful to manage as you work hard to overcome old habits. Good preparation and a kind supportiveness toward yourself are your best defenses.

1. Am I actively engaging in behaviors that are different from my old habit? Yes _____ No _____

2. Are others commenting on my change in behavior? Yes _____ No _____

Maintenance

The fifth stage of change, maintenance, is a time for solidifying progress. Your action plan has been implemented, and you are getting more familiar and comfortable with change. It is time to encounter people and situations that you avoided during the initial efforts to change. It is time to face temptation and to master it. Again, planning for the these encounters is the key to success. When taken by surprise, it's easy to lapse back into old coping behaviors. Expect problems to arise and have a new adaptive response ready.

In the past six months Vicky had been able to stick with her plan to remain at a job. Previously, she had worked a few days or weeks at a time before getting bored or angry and quitting. Her employment record was a shambles, which didn't make it easy for her to get a job she thought she would really like. Temporary work just wasn't bringing her the salary, benefits, and opportunity she wanted. She decided to change, and she put together her plan. She set a goal of one year of steady employment, marked days off on a calendar, rewarded herself each week for success and turned to her friends for support. Vicky is starting to relax a little and feels increasingly confident about her ability to succeed. She knows, though, to guard against overconfidence, since that often leads to careless mistakes. The past six months have been relatively stable for Vicky. She knows, too, that sudden or extra stress could threaten her success. She is prepared with a plan to manage crises and can call on her friends for support if needed.

The maintenance period is a time to be aware of possible pitfalls and to be sure you have a plan to handle them. It's also important to be respectful of the change process. Taking your success for granted is a setup for relapse. The maintenance stage can last from six months to a lifetime. Some people continue to encounter new situations that require adjustments in their action plan. Others find that they are handling the stress—expected and unexpected—both and move on to the termination stage.

1. Do I feel cocky or overconfident about my success to date?   Yes _____   No _____

2. Do I continue to practice techniques in my action plan?   Yes _____   No _____

3. Am I ready to renew my commitment to change?   Yes _____   No _____

Termination

The ideal of every self-change plan is to reach the termination stage. This final stage is marked by the absence of temptation to engage in the old way of behaving.

After two years of hard work, Christine had reached the termination stage of change. She has worked as hard as she could to overcome her impulsive speech patterns. In the past she interrupted others, blurted out obscenities, and spoke her mind to more than one supervisor. The problem, of course, brought plenty of trouble for her, including a few lost jobs. Christine succumbed to these conversation stoppers when she felt anxiety. She has learned to manage her fears with relaxation therapy, yoga, and regular aerobic exercise. Christine's confidence bloomed as she learned to control herself. She has not encountered an unmanageable situation for over a year.

Reaching the termination stage is a very individual journey. Prochaska and colleagues report that, for example, it takes from thirty-six to forty-eight months for smokers to reach the termination stage. But it will be different for each person attempting the change process. It will also vary for the behavior to be changed.

Relapses are a common phenomenon in the self-change process. *Relapse* has a harsh sound, suggesting failure, and Prochaska prefers to call the occurrence of slipping back a stage or two *recycling*. He and his colleagues report that it is highly likely that the process will not be smooth. Change rarely proceeds in a straight line from precontemplation to termination. Rather, recycling through the stages is to be expected. They report that 85 percent of smokers do not succeed in quitting on the first try. Regardless of how determined you are to overcome the habit, slipping back is most likely to occur when stress is high. Successful change requires anticipating and managing stress and a willingness to try and try again until the termination stage is reached.

1. Do I no longer worry that I'll slip back to old habits? Yes _____ No _____

2. Can I face old temptations without danger of falling to them? Yes _____ No _____

3. Is my new behavior comfortable and routine? Yes _____ No _____

Sources of Support

Before you begin your self-change effort, decide what kind of support you need from others and how you will get it. Adults with ADD are known to have poor self-observation skills. It is important that you find someone who can give you constructive feedback as well as encourage you in your goals to learn about new habits. Ed Hallowell and John Ratey emphasize the importance of a *coach* in your effort to learn about and to manage ADD. Others have noted the usefulness of support groups. A good support group can serve the purpose of educating you about ADD and providing encouragement for change. Finally, a therapist may be needed for particularly difficult problems.

Answer the following questions about your current available support. At the end of the section, choose the support(s) you will need for your own self-change to take effect.

Finding a Coach

Many individuals with ADD are reluctant to work with others on their self-change plan. People with ADD are often independent types who, like pioneers, want to blaze their own trails. It seems a burden to slow down and respond to the input from others. Also, the person with ADD likely has a long history of negative feedback. Working with a coach feels

1. Do I have someone to talk to about my feelings, problems, and plans? Yes _____ No _____

2. Do I have someone who understands and encourages me? Yes _____ No _____

3. Do I have an ongoing source of information about adult ADD? Yes _____ No _____

4. Do I have someone to contact if I need emergency assistance in dealing with temptations or problems? Yes _____ No _____

5. Do I feel comfortable listening and talking about personal problems in a group? Yes _____ No _____

like opening yourself up to a lot of criticism. It seems painful, too, to reveal shortcomings and admit the need for assistance.

With careful selection of your coach, the experience does not need to be painful. It's important to select your supportive other for the qualities of patience, honesty, kindness and objectivity. This is a pretty tall order, and most people will fall short on some of the qualities some of the time. But if you work with someone whom you fundamentally trust, you will likely feel good about the feedback you receive.

Your coach also should be someone you have easy access to. You will want to be able to get feedback on a frequent basis and be able to talk over potential problems. A spouse or significant other often can fulfill the role of coach, but you may feel more comfortable working with a close friend or roommate. If the problems associated with ADD have seriously strained a relationship, it may be a better choice to work with someone independent of these problems.

It's important to begin the relationship with a frank discussion of expectations. Let your coach know how often you would like to meet or if you want a more informal system of getting together. Let your coach know how to best give you constructive feedback. Identify for your coach any phrases that you've become overly sensitive to, and specify how you don't want to hear certain kinds of feedback. Then ask your coach for his or her feedback on the same issues.

When working with your coach, be an active participant. Clarify the feedback you are receiving if any point is unclear. Ask questions, but make your questions as specific as possible. Rather than asking, "How did I do?" ask, "How do you feel when I said . . . ?" or, "How could I have been clearer when . . . ?" You will learn far more in your feedback sessions if you direct your inquiries this way rather than talking in generalities.

Sometimes even well-timed, kindly expressed feedback is hard to hear. Try not to react in an angry, defensive manner. If you are put off by your coach's comments, you are likely to shut down dialogue and miss an opportunity to learn important information. If you react angrily often, you will effectively terminate the coaching relationship and find your efforts to change more difficult.

Backed by the best of intentions, your coach may occasionally push you to action when you are not ready. Again, people often mistake action for change. But change only occurs when action is preceded by good preparation. Do not let anyone push you to act until you have adequately prepared your plan.

Finding a Support Group

Joining a support group can be one of your easiest and most effective steps toward change. Support groups have been around for decades, modeling the success of Alcoholics Anonymous. AA was one of the earliest programs to use peer support in changing habits.

Support groups can give you feedback on your problems with managing ADD. You will find that others have faced similar problems, and you can learn new, innovative ways of managing ADD symptoms. You will find, too, that you have ideas and support to contribute. Helping others can be a major confidence booster when you feel you are struggling to manage problems of your own. While giving and getting ideas is extremely useful, the camaraderie of a group will likely be the biggest return on your investment of time. A number of studies show that support group participants consistently acknowledge the sense of community with others sharing the same problems as the most important benefit of belonging.

The makeup of support groups will vary with the group. The formats, memberships, meeting times and places will differ depending on group composition. If you have the opportunity, attend a few groups and select the one that feels best for you. Look for mature, supportive participants and good leadership that does not permit members to be pressured into action until ready.

There are now support groups for adults with ADD in most states and large cities. If you are not yet a member of a group, check the phone book, or with your physician or local mental health clinic for a group in your area. You also can contact one of the following national ADD groups for adults to get a list of groups available to you.

Attention Deficit Disorder Association (ADDA)
P.O. Box 488
West Newbury, MA 01985

C.H.A.D.D.
(Children and Adults with Attention Deficit Disorder)
499 NW 70th Avenue, #308
Plantation, FL 33317
305-587-3700

Adult Attention Deficit Foundation
132 North Woodward Avenue
Birmingham, MI 48009
313-540-6335

Attention Deficit Resource Center
1344 Johnson Ferry Road, #14
Marietta, GA 30068
800-537-3784

Adult ADD Association
1225 East Sunset Drive, #640
Bellingham, WA 98226-3529
206-647-6681

ADDult News
c/o Mary Jane Johnson
2620 Ivy Place
Toledo, OH 43613

Forming Support Groups

If there is no support group near you, or you don't feel comfortable in the ones you attend, consider forming your own. The essence of a support group is that individuals with a similar problem share experiences, information, and encouragement. With some preparation, and focused energy, you can create this environment for yourself and other adults with ADD. It's natural for a group to have a leader. If you have someone available to you who has experience leading a support group, it's a good idea to accept this expertise. If an experienced leader is not available, group members can fulfill this role with some guidelines. It's best to rotate the leadership function on a meeting-to-meeting basis so that members feel equally valued. In addition, rotating the leadership will give every member some practice at being a leader in a setting where the other members of the group are like-minded, and can give valuable, specific feedback.

To get the group started, you'll need to make plans in a number of areas. Contacting an existing ADD support group is a useful way to learn a number of points about start-up.

- You will need to decide how to recruit members. Newspaper ads and posters on bulletin boards (paper and computer) at school, community notice boards, and libraries are good places to start. You may also be able to post signs at local mental health clinics and send notices to mental health workers. Radio and TV stations and cable channels (especially at night) may run your ad as a public service announcement. Just list the places would go for information if you were looking for a group.

- Determine a meeting place. If you are meeting with friends and neighbors, a member's home may be appropriate. If the members do not know one another, a church, community center, or library setting may be more comfortable and secure.

- Determine group membership. Six to eight persons is recommended. Larger groups inhibit the flow of communication and greatly reduce the amount of individual attention members can receive. In a one-hour meeting, eight members would get about seven minutes of attention each.

- Some groups meet for an undetermined length of time; others limit the time. As a group, you may decide to meet for general discussions and support or you may want to focus on specific tasks. You could use this workbook to give a structure and purpose to your group.

- If you decide to limit the time, one and a half to two hours is recommended. Take breaks, too. People with ADD will appreciate the opportunity to move around.

- Rules for confidentiality should be established and agreed to by each member joining the group. Members should agree not to mention other members by name outside of the group and not to discuss members' personal issues with nonmembers.

- Other ground rules are important, too. Members should respect each others' current stage of change. No one should feel forced to take action without good preparation and commitment. Each member needs to feel understood and respected. Teasing, criticism, or disinterest by others must not be allowed.

- Each member should be able to share experiences at each meeting if desired. It can be a difficult task to be sure that everyone who wants to can speak. This need must be balanced with the need for members not to be incomplete in communicating personal experiences. Someone needs to keep one eye on the clock and respectfully keep the discussion moving.

The support you receive from a group can be very gratifying. Through this experience you can lose the sense of isolation of coping with ADD. Your defenses can become less rigid, and you will free up energy that can be directed at the real work of learning—mastering ADD.

Finding a Therapist

An alternative (or adjunct) to working with a coach and support group is to find professional help. Working with a therapist may be a difficult step for an adult with ADD to take. For years others have said that there is something wrong with you. And with the pressure of managing ADD in this world, you may have wondered about your mental health, too. Seeking professional help may seem like an admission of failure.

Movies, TV, and sometimes the press often conjure up images of therapy that are largely false. You need not worry that you will be lying on a couch talking about your mother for years to come. A good therapist serves more as an advisor. Someone with perspective and experience can help you to quickly discover how you want to handle your problem. Today therapy is usually short-term and problem-focused.

There are many good reasons to decide to seek professional help:

- You are engaging in dangerous or destructive behaviors such as excessive drinking, unsafe sexual practices, or compulsive behaviors such as gambling, overeating, or shopping.

- You have had frequent or serious setbacks when implementing your own change programs.

- Your problems are long-term and resistant to your efforts to change.

- You have insufficient supports to assist you in your effort to change, such as family, friends, or access to a support group.

- New problems seem to occur as soon as you have effectively changed an old one.

• Your problems seem to recur despite your best efforts to prevent them.

To find a therapist, you may start by asking your physician for a referral. Ask your friends, too, for a recommendation to a therapist they may have seen. Very often a therapist who worked successfully with a friend can be helpful to you. Also, you can talk with your friend about the therapist's style and rule out some possibilities even before an initial meeting. Try to settle on two or three names, and then make a single appointment to see each of them. In the initial interview, the therapist will ask a lot of questions regarding the history of your problem and your efforts to cope. You should also ask questions. Ask about the therapist's style and experience with your problem. Also ask about the structure of the therapy sessions and how long you would expect to work together. Be attuned to the therapist's interpersonal skills. You want to select someone who is honest, caring, and patient.

Summary

• Change is a process that occurs in six stages:

1. Precontemplation: Change is avoided and problems are denied.
2. Contemplation: The need for change is accepted and information about a problem is sought.
3. Preparation: Plans for change are made.
4. Action: The plan for change is implemented.
5. Maintenance: Success is solidified.
6. Termination: New behaviors become habits and efforts to change can stop.

Exercise

Now that you have read about the possible sources of support, list below the supportive relationships you will use throughout your change program.

_____

_____

_____

_____

_____

- Having supportive people in your life is important for change. There are many ways to find the support you need:

    Coach: A friend, spouse, or roommate may be a coach. Choose someone who is honest and kind. Clarify your expectations at the beginning.

    Support group: Meet with a group of people who share similar problems and experiences with ADD. Support groups should provide encouragement and respect for the individual.

    Therapist: This may be an alternative or adjunct to a coach and support group. Find a therapist to work with if your ADD issues are threatening your health or safety.

4

Self-Esteem:

Put Criticism in Its Place

Holding yourself in high regard is essential for leading a satisfactory life. People with ADD often have marvelous gifts of spontaneity and creativity. They can be sensitive and can quickly and accurately assess the motives of others. People with ADD are successful as artists, doctors, inventors, and businesspeople. Yet high numbers of adults with ADD suffer from low self-esteem. Thomas Whiteman reports that 40 percent of ADD adults under his treatment have low self-esteem.

Thirty-two-year-old Rick, an engineer, can build, fix, program, and install computers with ease. He's also tall, has better than average looks, and he's plagued with self-doubt. He got through school by putting himself on a rigid study schedule. He never conquered his ADD problem with social relationships though. He was never comfortable around the guys in school and feels he failed at "locker-room humor." He doesn't feel he has much chance with the opposite sex either. He forgets his dates' names and often talks a mile-a-minute about his wide-ranging but esoteric interests. He avoids really interesting women since he feels doomed to fail. He's not happy with his life's direction.

Self-esteem is composed of the statements you make to yourself about your abilities, worth, and status. If you feel that you have few talents, that you are not lovable, and that you're never going to get anywhere, your self-esteem will be low. Self-esteem also is measured by the situations you seek for yourself. If you repeatedly put yourself in situations where you will be mistreated or hurt by others, your self-esteem will suffer.

Self-esteem develops in childhood. Your parents and teachers gave you feedback about what was good and bad according to their value systems. As a child with ADD, you likely had lots of energy and found yourself in trouble frequently. The message sent to you was that you were difficult. Developing friendships also was problematic due to your impulsivity. Parents, teachers, siblings, and friends may not have been careful to balance their negative feedback with a large, healthy dose of positive reinforcement. As a result, you may have struggled with issues of self-esteem for your entire life.

Exercise

Answer the following questions:

1. I feel that I am attractive. Yes _____ No _X___

2. I think I have talent in one or more areas. Yes _____ No _X___

3. I feel pretty inept a lot of the time. Yes _____ No _____

4. I often think I'll never get ahead. Yes X_____ No _____

5. I have important relationships in which I am hurt in some way. Yes X_____ No _____

6. I feel I have major physical flaws. Yes X_____ No _____

7. I feel that I am lovable. Yes _____ No _____

8. I feel that I have good social status. Yes _____ No X_____

9. I feel that I am an intelligent person. Yes _X___ No _____

10. I feel that I'm not well liked by others. Yes X_____ No _____

If you answered yes to questions 3, 4, 5, 6, or 10 or no to questions 1, 2, 7, 8, or 9, you have problems with self-esteem in these areas.

How the Internal Critic Operates

An internal voice tells you, "You didn't push hard enough," "You're hopelessly disorganized," "You never follow through," "You're late, as always," "You messed up again." This voice is your internal critic talking. It's a voice that evaluates your thoughts, feelings, and actions. The critic has a perfect memory. It can recount every mistake you've ever made, enumerate your every flaw, and list every disappointment you have ever had. Everyone has an internal critic. Some critics are relatively quiet, except during times of stress. Others are obnoxiously loud and present all the time. The critic destroys self-esteem. For every step forward that you take, it will push you two steps back. The critic develops in childhood. It has internalized all of the negative feedback you've heard from parents, teachers, and friends. Your critic has been with you so long you may not even recognize its voice. You are so used to hearing its criticism that you take it for granted. The critic can switch on automatically. These automatic thoughts are causing your anxiety and self-doubt.

As toxic as the critic is, it did develop as a way to protect you. If the critic can put you down first, it will be less painful when others do so. The critic also tries to alert you to the possibility of failure, again so that you won't be surprised and stung. The problem with this defense is that it exchanges long-term love of self for the short-term comfort. Your critic may lessen the pain of an immediate experience, but in the long run, you accept these negative statements and make them part of your belief system.

The Principle of Reinforcement

Habits develop as a result of reinforcement. The principle of reinforcement states that acts that are rewarded will be repeated when circumstances are similar. This simple principle shapes a great deal of our behavior. Consider your everyday actions. You are more likely to smile at those who smile back at you. You are more likely to play games when you have a chance at winning. Thoughts, like behavior, are shaped by reinforcement. Thoughts that are rewarded are more likely to be repeated.

Reinforcement may be either positive or negative. Positive reinforcement occurs when an act is followed by a positive event. You return a lost wallet and receive a reward. Or you wish someone you like would call, and he does. Your wishing behavior will likely increase following this event. Some behavior of the critic also may be positively reinforced. The critic sometimes serves to spur you on to greater achievement. By whipping you to try harder, work faster, and so on, it may sometimes get you to accomplish more. Because your caustic thinking was then rewarded with achievement, you are likely to repeat this type of thinking. You may even come to believe that this mental beratement is the *only* way to get yourself going.

The critic is also motivated by negative reinforcement. Behavior is likely to be repeated when it is rewarded by the termination of some negative event. If you have a headache and take an aspirin, you will soon experience relief. This is negative reinforcement. Also, if you're building up frustration and blow off steam by yelling at your spouse, you may experience tension reduction, and this relief is negative reinforcement. You'll be likely to yell again when you're feeling tense.

The internal critic is often maintained by the principle of negative reinforcement. The critic can serve to reduce a number of negative feelings, such as anxiety, frustration, and doubt.

> Fredericka is 28 and recently divorced. She consoled herself many nights throughout the separation from her husband by baking and eating. She has put on a few extra pounds. Fredericka now thinks about meeting men and starting a relationship. The thoughts bring her to near panic. She thinks about "how awful" she looks and decides not to try to go out for a while. She immediately feels relief.

Fredericka's self-critical remarks worked—at least for the moment—and her tension is reduced. In many similar ways the critic prevents or prepares you for failure and thereby lessens the blow.

Conquering the Internal Critic

Over the years, self-criticism becomes a habitual way of thinking. Fortunately, the pattern can be reversed. Habit control procedures can be applied to negative thought processes as well as other behaviors, such as smoking, nail-biting, and overeating. A three-step program of awareness, thought-stopping, and alternative thinking can overcome this bad habit.

Develop Your Awareness of the Critic

Awareness is a first step in changing your thinking habits. Because the critic developed in childhood and is very well ingrained, you may not be aware when the critic is up and operating. To take this first essential step, you must begin to listen to your own thoughts. Keeping a daily log is recommended. The log will help you to focus attention on the task and facilitate memory. Also, the log will give you an idea of just how powerful your critic is. By keeping a log, you'll see on a daily basis how frequently you are putting yourself down. Initially, you may make very few entries. But as you become increasingly attuned to your internal critic, you're likely be amazed at how many of its insults you endure each day.

Exercise

Copy the Internal Critic Log form on the following page, and record your thoughts on a daily basis.

Practice this for at least a week before you take the next step in the habit control plan. Only after you have developed a real awareness of when and how your critic operates will you be in a position to stop its effect. Here are a few examples of typical self-critical thoughts:

Time	Critical Thought
4:10 p.m.	Why can't I find my car keys? How stupid can I be?
6:30 p.m.	I never follow through on anything.
9:30 p.m.	I give in too easily.

Practice Thought-Stopping

When you catch yourself engaging in the bad habit of self-criticism, you need to stop immediately. As mentioned before, if you practice any behavior and it has a rewarding value, you strengthen it, and it's likely to be repeated again and again. As soon as you identify your self-critical thought, make a statement such as, "No, I'm not putting myself down." If the thought continues, you may need a stronger signal, such as loudly saying, "*Stop.*" You can say

Internal Critic Log

Day _____   Date _____

Time   Critical Thought

_____   _____

_____   _____

_____   _____

_____   _____

_____   _____

_____   _____

_____   _____

_____   _____

_____   _____

_____   _____

_____   _____

_____   _____

_____   _____

_____   _____

_____   _____

_____   _____

_____   _____

_____   _____

this to yourself, of course, if you are with others. Another form of thought-stopping is to wear a rubber band around your wrist and to snap it each time you have a critical thought. The sting of the band will temporarily distract you from your self-criticism.

Replace Critical Thoughts with Alternative Thoughts

The third step of habit control is to replace the stopped, self-critical thought with a self-affirming thought. If you've stopped yourself from saying, "You idiot," you can replace the negative thought with, "You're trying your best. Keep it up." It's important that the thought you stop is replaced by a related but positive alternative. Consider the following examples:

Self-Criticism	Self-Affirmation
I'm always late.	I'm on time some of the time.
I'm sloppy.	I'm being as careful as I can.
I'm lazy.	I get a lot of things done.

Alternative thoughts should be related to the criticism, and they should be accurate reflections of who you are and what you're doing *now*. If you answer the critic by saying what you hope to be (for example, "Some day I'll get organized"), you're acknowledging the critic's point. Instead, make an affirmation of yourself in the present, such as, "I'm better organized

Exercise

Write self-affirmations for the critical comments below.

Self-criticism: There you go again. You always give up.

Self-affirmation: _____

Self-criticism: You should have started earlier.

Self-affirmation: _____

Self-criticism: You just can't seem to get it.

Self-affirmation: _____

Self-criticism: You are such a klutz.

Self-affirmation: _____

Self-criticism: You are so stupid.

Self-affirmation: _____

than I used to be" or "I've started to use a daily schedule." Specific thoughts help you to focus on your hard work in the present. Also, as these thoughts help to reduce the tension preceding the self-criticism, they will negatively reinforce your self-affirmation. With repeated practice, you'll be able to soothe yourself and relieve tension in a constructive way.

Handling Criticism from Others

While the internal critic attacks you from within, sources outside yourself may criticize you as well. School reports state, "could do better," bosses rant about work not finished, and friends, spouses, and parents complain about your lateness, interrupting, forgetting, and so on. These seemingly never-ending complaints from all sides can give your self-esteem a hammering.

Criticism can stem from a genuine desire to help. When caring is the motivation, the feedback will take a specific form and be accurate; for example, when your date says, "You're about an hour late. I'd like you to be on time." However, criticism is all too often delivered with an angry punch, such as when your date meets you at the door with, "You're hours late. You're the most inconsiderate, selfish person I've ever met." Such angry, inaccurate comments reflect the emotional experiences of the speaker. It's likely that your date has been stood up by someone who was selfish and insensitive. Your lateness stirs those old fears that this relationship will be a bad experience, too. You are taken by surprise at the door with this barrage, and your old feelings get aroused. Confrontation follows, and the social event fizzles.

The experience of being criticized is complex. It may contain an element of surprise, as in the previous example. You hear a grain of truth in the comment. You relate it to past, similar experiences and fear the outcome. You also feel the aggression of the anger. It's confusing, and you're not sure what to react to first. In this confusion, you may rely on old defenses, such as impulsively striking back or letting your internal critic turn against you.

Exercise

Think of a recent experience of criticism you have had. Write it below as accurately and completely as you can.

_____

_____

_____

_____

_____

_____

The following sections look at different ways of responding constructively to criticism. The goal is to develop healthy defenses to these attacks. Working through an actual recent experience with criticism will make the process more real and useful to you.

Assess the Critism and Practice New Responses

Getting a good assessment of the criticism is the first step to responding in a constructive way. Accurate assessment requires a cool head—rational, objective consideration of the comments. To trigger assessment, you will need a signal for the process to begin. People with ADD are often good at visualization. You may, for example, practice seeing a flashing STOP sign over the head of the person criticizing you. Or, imagine seeing red flags pop out of your critic's ears or head. These signs tell you to stop and think. No automatic responses allowed. When the assessment process is triggered, quickly ask yourself, "Is it true?" When criticism is accurate, acknowledge the fact. When you state, "Yes, I was an hour late," the critic is stopped. You are, after all, agreeing. Whatever emotion was behind the remark also will usually come to a sputtering stop. It's also likely that your critic is only partially accurate. Criticism that is fueled by emotion is overblown. It can be full of sarcasm and innuendo. The task in this case is to pick out the part of the message that is accurate or might be accurate under some circumstances.

Here are some examples of responses that acknowledge the critic without buying into the emotion:

Supervisor: Your office is a disaster. You lose everything. Just last week you lost the figures for the sales project.

Employee: You're right. I did lose those numbers.

Professor: You're not trying hard enough. If you keep handing in papers like this, you'll flunk out of here.

Student: You're right. I could flunk out.

Exercise

Consider the following examples of criticism, and write an acknowledging response.

1. What's the matter with you? You're not paying any attention to what you wear. You can't wear a blue sweater with green pants and brown socks. Are you color-blind?

_____

_____

_____

2. Can't you get a handle on your money? You'll always be broke. You just never think before you act.

_____

_____

_____

3. Don't you ever think of the consequences of your behavior? You could have lost a friend that way.

_____

_____

_____

Here is one more example:

Customer: You're not paying any attention to what I've said.

Waiter: You're right. I've been distracted. How can I help you?

Inaccurate Criticism

There are times when you can find no point of agreement with your critic. Lack of any mutual ground occurs when the criticism is untrue or completely vague.

Charles faced a tirade from his anxious, exhausted wife. She arrived home from the grocery store and said, "You never once think of anyone but yourself. You're trying to wear me out and keep us broke so I can't leave. But if your inconsiderate habits keep up, I'm leaving." Charles was surprised, to say the least, and didn't know where or how to begin to respond. His wife's criticism mentioned no specific act but accused him of destructive motivation.

Verbal tantrums from another adult can be maddening. But if your signal system is working, you'll see red flags all over the place. You can then, mentally, take a step back and begin to neutralize the situation.

When falsely accused, ask questions. Ask for a specific instance of the behavior described. Ask for examples of the motivation ascribed to you. Remember, you're looking for information and trying to neutralize the situation, so keeping your own emotional tone in control is important. If you feel that the situation tolerates it, you can also correct misinformation of your critic. Charles might say to his wife, "I'm not trying to wear you out. In fact, I worry that you're working too hard."

Exercise

Write a response to the following criticisms. Keep the response rational and emotionally neutral.

1. You're a mess. You never finish anything. You'll never amount to anything.

_____

_____

_____

2. You're such a klutz. You're deliberately trying to destroy this place with all your antics.

_____

_____

_____

3. Loser.

_____

_____

_____

To Err Is Human

No one likes to make mistakes, but we all do. If we could accept mistakes as a human foible, there would be no problem and no relationship between mistakes and self-esteem. Self-esteem often suffers, though, when making a mistake is equated with your worth. This problem typically originates in childhood when a significant person, parent, or teacher points out an error that you made and then goes beyond the simple slip in behavior to characterize you in a negative way for having made it. Statements like "You're so clumsy, you broke the flowerpot," or "Why can't you pay attention? You're spilling the milk all over the table," do more than point out a mistake, they put down the person making it. Over time, you learn to see your mistakes as a measure of your worth.

A mistake is any action that you later regret. The key word here is _later_. It is not a mistake at the time you made it. It was the best decision you could make with the information

Exercise

Reconsider your own experience with criticism that you recorded earlier in the chapter, and answer the following questions.

1. Was it untrue? Yes _____ No _____

    If yes, write a response to correct the misconception.

    _____

    _____

    _____

2. Were you falsely accused of destructive motivation? Yes _____ No _____

    If yes, write a response to clarify your intentions.

    _____

    _____

    _____

Exercise

Choose a mistake that you have made recently, and write it down here. Your mistake can be big or small. In later exercises, you will apply the techniques in this section to that mistake as practice for learning how to manage this inevitable human experience.

_____

_____

_____

_____

you had at the time. Remembering that you did not set out to make a mistake, that you were trying to do the best you could under the circumstance, is an important way to neutralize the critic when things do not turn out as you planned.

When results are different from our expectations, we often lament, "If only I had done . . ." Hindsight is often said to be twenty-twenty. But it is *not*. If you had chosen another path, unforeseen results could have occured, and there is no guarantee that it would have worked out better than the decision you made.

Advantages of Mistakes

We regret decisions when we feel that we have lost out on some important gain. The focus is on the loss. It may be surprising to realize that mistakes have their advantages, too. While the loss is usually felt immediately (or in the short-term), the advantages of your mistakes are related to your long-term gain.

Learning

Mistakes can be instructive. At the time of your decision, you incorporated the best information you had. Since that time, additional information became available. Attending to the new input and incorporating it into future decisions will increase your effectiveness. If, however, you focus on your loss and engage in self-beratement, you'll not attend to recent developments and will likely repeat previous decisions.

Learning necessarily involves making mistakes. Imagine learning to play the piano without ever missing a note, or learning to drive without hitting the brakes too hard at least once. Only when you are willing to be wrong can learning occur. This is not to endorse a trial-and-error approach to learning or impulsively going off in any direction. But giving yourself the freedom to practice and fail is necessary.

Warnings

Mistakes also serve as warnings that something requires your attention. If your boss sends back your monthly report with a number of errors flagged, you could get angry with his pickiness or berate yourself for sloppy work. You also could take this information as a warning that something went wrong during the month when you prepared the report. Were you too rushed or tired? You can then make adjustments in your work schedule to avoid future last-minute problems.

Humility

An advantage of making a mistake is that it can sometimes lead you to a healthy respect for what you're trying to accomplish. It can also help you to appreciate those who have attempted the task before you. It is so often the case that when adults with ADD become parents, they find out how hard it is to be patient with a hyperactive child. This revelation sometimes results in the adult with ADD becoming more supportive toward a spouse, boss, or friend who has to tolerate ADD in others.

Spontaneity

Feeling free to make mistakes can lead to an increased involvement in life. Giving yourself permission to make mistakes is liberating. You increase your opportunities to learn and to experience novelty.

Exercise

Identify the advantages of the mistake you made.

1. What did you learn? _____

_____

2. In what ways did it serve as a warning? _____

_____

3. How did it give you greater respect for the job and others? _____

_____

4. How did it free you to experience life? _____

_____

Attention and Mistakes

Most mistakes are made due to inattention. As an adult with ADD you've probably been told, "What were you thinking? Couldn't you see what was coming? You've got to wake up. You've missed the point entirely." Receiving a barrage of these statements and others like them over many formative years can lead to lowered self-esteem.

As adults these comments are particularly frustrating since you're aware that you have difficulty maintaining attention. And it's discouraging to feel you have let yourself down again. The problem with the criticism from yourself and others is that it's not instructive. There are different types and reasons for inattention, and it's helpful to know how they lead to mistakes.

Forgetting

Problems with memory are common in people with ADD. Even without ADD, no one can remember all of the experiences, decisions, and results of a lifetime. It is inevitable that relevant information will be forgotten. You are particularly likely to forget experiences that are not very intense or positive, and to remember experiences that are very happy or very sad. Therefore these intense, emotional experiences are more accessible when similar situations arise.

Habit

Almost by definition, we do not attend to habitual behavior. Habits are often automatic ways of behaving. But habits can lead to mistakes when circumstances change and you haven't noticed. If you're used to driving to work one way, for example, and you don't notice signs for future road work, you can find yourself very late one day when a detour is necessary. As another example, a young woman habitually talked incessantly about personal information (surgeries, phobias) on her first dates. Men were most often turned off and didn't ask her out again. She couldn't see that her interpersonal communication style was costing her the social life she craved.

Denial

This is a very strong form of inattention that is based on self-protection. Acknowledging the existence of a problem is too threatening to the self. Refusing to admit to a problem avoids this frightening experience for a while.

Kathy, never diagnosed with ADD, drinks excessively every day. Drinking helps her to forget the lost sale at work that day, soothe her over the argument with her husband, and give her courage to talk back to her sales manager. But Kathy has traded those problems for the destruction of her health and lowering of her self-esteem through reliance on a crutch.

When analyzed for their components of loss and inattention and seen from a new perspective of their advantages, mistakes are more understandable. Understanding yourself is

Exercise

Consider the mistake you have made recently. How was it a result of:

1. Forgetting: _____

_____

2. Habit: _____

_____

3. Denial: _____

_____

the first step in acceptance. And, when you accept and forgive yourself, you are building self-esteem.

Quieting your internal critic and handling and accepting mistakes will improve your self-esteem. You will have greater understanding, acceptance, and kindness for yourself. For a further reading and practice on the topic of self-esteem, we recommend Matt McKay and Pat Fanning's excellent, thorough treatment of the subject in their book, *Self-Esteem.*

Summary

- Self-esteem develops in childhood from the feedback you receive from parents, teachers, siblings, friends, and others. Children with ADD commonly receive a lot of negative feedback; thus, as adults, they very often have problems with lowered self-esteem.

- An internal critic develops as results of criticism received during your formative years.

- The critic is so practiced that it switches on automatically and may go unnoticed. Although it is trying to protect you from hurt, it is sacrificing long-term satisfaction for short-term comfort.

- A three-step program of awareness, thought-stopping, and alternative self-affirmations can bring your internal critic under control.

- Handling criticism from others can also be a problem. When criticized by others, stop an automatic response and give yourself time to think. Also, learn to assess whether the criticism is accurate or not and if you can acknowledge part of it.

- Making mistakes often decreases self-esteem, but they are less devastating when you realize that they have advantages, such as facilitating learning and providing warning signals. It also helps to know that mistakes are often a result of inattention, forgetting, habit, and denial.

5

Rational Thinking:

Get a Handle on Automatic Thoughts

Depression is a frequently cited problem in ADD. While people with ADD are often intelligent, energetic, and imaginative, they have difficulty developing the skills needed to work with others, such as organization, follow-through, and social finesse. People with ADD have likely received much criticism from others and have failed in many settings by the time they reach adulthood. Depression can result from this lengthy struggle with frustration and failure.

The National Institute of Mental Health estimates that 20 percent of the population experience depression at some point in life. Depression is highly treatable. There are new, effective medications, and extensive research has shown that behavior therapy is a powerful technique for alleviating depression.

In the 1960s Aaron Beck pioneered a form of behavior therapy that deals specifically with the problem of depression. Dr. Beck noted that it is often your thoughts that trigger depressed feelings. How you interpret events determines how you feel about them. If you interpret your boss's stiff "Hello" as a sign of annoyance at your late report, you will feel anxious. If you interpret it as his usual absentmindedness, you will feel neutral.

Dr. Beck noted that people jump to a conclusion, and that provokes emotions. Because the interpretations are quick in coming, he called them *automatic thoughts*. He noted, too, that these thoughts are sometimes just a flash of memory related to an experience. Automatic thoughts are ingrained, based on past experience, quick, and sometimes abbreviated to just a visual memory.

Cognitive Distortions and Their Role in Depression

Automatic thoughts are also called cognitive distortions. These are statements you make to yourself that distort your emotions and experiences. Because they are automatic, you rarely notice or examine them. You accept them as truths. Although they are based on experience, it is false to extend them to the present without first examining their validity.

This chapter examines ten common cognitive distortions. It shows you how to uncover the fallacies in each and how to overcome the negative emotions and distractions that result.

Filtering

Filtering is the process of putting your experiences through a mental strainer that separates only the negative aspects.

> Nigel works hard at his job as a photographer. His ADD is not a handicap in his work because he can be constantly on the go and he can use his visual imagination. Nigel's boss is "all business." He met Nigel at the studio one morning and gave him two important assignments for the day. He told Nigel to be sure to have them in on time. Nigel left brooding over his boss's admonition to "have them in on time." He felt he was being criticized and it was unfair. Nigel isolated this one statement and put it through a filter of injustice, leaving him angry for the day.

We each select filters based on our personal history. If you are depressed, you will filter out elements of loss in your experiences. People who are fearful will see danger in what they encounter. What is filtered may be real, but it's a distortion of the total experience because it's only *one* aspect of what happened. Nigel did not see that he had been given two important assignments, which would suggest trust on his boss's part. Nigel could have left the studio feeling pretty proud.

Catastrophizing

Linking your present situation to a disastrous conclusion is catastrophizing. You feel that the worst outcome will befall you. If you have a cold, you worry that it will turn into pneumonia. If you run out of gas on the highway, you're sure you'll be hijacked—even killed. People with ADD are susceptible to catastrophizing since they often feel that doom is just around the corner. Also, because of their active imaginations, they can dream up the most amazing outcomes for ordinary situations.

Catastrophizing takes a lot of time and energy that could otherwise be used to deal with the original situation. Catastrophizing also creates negative emotions, usually anxiety. Once generated, anxiety is associated with the current situation and then may recur automatically in the future.

Overgeneralization

Overgeneralization involves drawing a conclusion from one experience and extending this conclusion to all future experiences. For example, if you've had an unsuccessful interview and conclude you're a failure at interviewing and you'll never get a job, you're overgeneralizing. The result of one interview cannot determine how well you'll do in the future. Even if you have had several unsuccessful interviews, you're future has *not* been determined. All these interviews are independent of one another.

Similar conclusions, such as, "No one will ever go out with me," "I'll never get into grad school," "I'll always be in this rut of a job," and "Everything goes wrong for me," are gross overgeneralizations. Overgeneralizations result in a narrowing of your life experiences. As you conclude that failure is inevitable, you're less likely to challenge yourself.

Labeling

Being labeled is a common experience for someone with ADD. ADD itself is, of course, a label. Not everyone using the term understands that it is a collection of behaviors that can be used skillfully or destructively. Rather, the emphasis is on "deficit" and "disorder." You are certainly familiar with other labels, such as lazy, disorganized, immature. You know the hurt feelings that theses words cause. You know that hurt usually leads to anger and eventually depression.

Unfortunately, being labeled does not immunize you from using labels yourself. If you are breaking up with your boyfriend and refer to him as a "loser," you're engaging in the distortion of labeling. You are focusing on one or a few aspects of his character that displease you and using them to define him as a person. The result of labeling is that it distances you from the person. You can then more easily justify angry, aggressive behavior toward this person.

Mind Reading

Feeling that you just "know" how someone feels or will act is a form of projection called mind reading. You draw quick conclusions about others based on your feelings rather than real information.

Lois sat nervously across from her boss at the weekly staff meeting. She noted that he only made brief eye contact with her. Later he didn't support her suggestion to shorten the performance appraisal form. She concluded that he was not happy with her work and he wanted to fire her. The truth was, he had just come from a meeting with his boss and was preoccupied with his own job security.

In mind reading you know how you would feel about a situation and assume that others feel the same way you do. If you are annoyed when someone spills coffee in a restaurant, you feel that anyone else would feel annoyed as well. The problem with mind reading is that you will then act according to your beliefs about others' feelings or values. You may make yourself look pretty irrational by making up for something no one else perceived to be a problem.

Shoulds

"Shoulds" are statements that you make to yourself about how the world ought to be. You have ideas, experiences, values that indicate to you right from wrong. The problem comes when you apply these imperatives to day-to-day situations, and those who fail your expectations are wrong or bad. For example, you feel that your wife should know when you've had a bad day and need some time alone. When she does not, you feel that she is selfish and demanding. Or, you are cut off in traffic by a young man driving a sports car. Your blood boils as you say, "He shouldn't get away with that. He's a punk and should be run off the road." Obeying traffic laws is a good idea, but not everyone does. Your level of anger for his violation is extreme under the circumstances.

Shoulds can also be turned inward. You may have a number of rules for your own behavior. You may feel that you should be able to talk your way into any sale you want. Again, the problem with shoulds is the condemnation that comes with not meeting the standard. You feel that you're a weakling if you give in to not feeling well or that you're a failure when you can't close every sale you want. Shoulds are rigid and demanding. Psychologist Karen Horey calls them "the tyranny of the shoulds." These immutable, fixed beliefs keep you from flexible thinking and evaluation of yourself and others based on all of the present circumstances.

Personalization

Personalization is the belief that everything around you somehow relates to what you've done or said. If the cashier at the supermarket has a critical look on his face, you feel that he is judging you in some way. You don't stop to think that maybe he's preoccupied with some thought of his own. Or, if your boss gives a speech about increasing productivity, you're sure he's talking about you and that he's really looking to fire you. Personalization also makes you responsible for the well-being of others. If your son is sad, you feel that you must have let him down in some way.

Comparing yourself to others is another aspect of personalization. You are on the lookout for the abilities of others and compare their success to yours. You see others' ability to play tennis, sing, write, converse, and you feel that your talent is less. These comparisons are a constant search to establish your own value as a person. Occasionally, you may feel that you are the better-looking, smarter, happier person, but the success rarely lasts. You begin comparing yourself to others again and inevitably find others better off than you.

Polarized Thinking

Judging your experiences as either black or white, good or bad, is the essence of polarized thinking. You are not seeing the shades of gray.

Rose has experienced a lot of loss in her life. She finds it hard to trust people. When Rose's husband becomes preoccupied with a personal project, she feels abandoned and resentful. She sees her husband at these times as selfish and incompetent. He's a bad husband. She also feels that she must be pretty lousy as a wife if he's so uninterested in her.

Living with Attention Deficit Disorder

Rose is judging herself and her husband in black-and-white terms. Either he's a good husband or a bad husband. Similarly, she is either a good or bad wife.

Polarized thinking is critical and harsh. It's brittle, too. There is no room for mistakes. If you fail, you must be a failure. You're either brilliant or stupid, clever or a klutz. Because your experiences are anchored at the extremes, your emotions and your moods will swing between the poles. You experience a lot of mood variability and energy highs and lows.

Fairness

Fairness is something we all would like to be part of human relations. But people don't always agree on what is fair. The fallacy of fairness involves determining for yourself what is fair in a relationship and expecting others to share the same view. This fallacy is often expressed in "if, then" statements. "She knows I have ADD. She shouldn't expect me to be on time." "If we were a real family, they would come over on Sundays." "If they wanted me to stay, they would give me a raise."

A related fallacy of fairness involves setting a quid pro quo—but without letting others know the deal. For example, since you did all the cooking tonight, you feel that others should know to do the cleanup. Or, since you've been working extra hours to help with the new ad campaign, you should get your choice of vacation weeks. When others do not know your private agenda, you are likely to end up feeling let down. Without an open understanding, there is no agreement.

Control

The fallacy of control has two forms. In the first, you feel that others control your destiny. In the second, you feel that you are able to control the lives of others.

Feeling controlled by others or outside forces is a cause for discouragement. When you believe that outcomes are determined by others, rather than your talent or hard work, you may give up before you try. Fallacies of control by others are a major contributor to procrastination. For example, if you believe that East Coast schools won't consider Midwestern applicants, you have an excuse not to try.

The second type of control fallacy is that you can control the lives, behavior, and/or feelings of others. You are then responsible for their outcomes. This much responsibility can be a real burden. Living with someone who procrastinates sometimes results in this type of thinking. You feel that it is somehow your responsibility, your duty, to get them to change their ways, to get moving, and to do what's right. This is a fallacy. You cannot control another's behavior or feelings. Even when the person agrees with you and does what you ask, it's a result of that person's decision.

Ten Fallacies of Thinking

Here is a summary of the ten cognitive distortions:

- Filtering: You see only the negative aspects of an experience; you disregard positive and neutral aspects.

- Catastrophizing: You can see eventual disaster in any everyday experience.

Rational Thinking

- Overgeneralization: You extrapolate from one or a few experiences to all future experiences.

- Labeling: You use a word or a phrase to define an entire person.

- Mind reading: You make quick decisions about what others are thinking without actual evidence.

- Shoulds: You have a set of rules for the behavior of others and yourself. When the rules are broken, you feel angry and judge the violation as bad.

- Personalization: You feel that all events around you somehow reflect on you. You feel responsible for the well-being of others.

- Polarized thinking: You see your experiences in black-and-white terms. You are either good or bad, smart or dumb, and so on.

- Fairness: You have a standard of fairness that others must follow. You always have hidden agreements about what others should do for you to reward your efforts.

- Control: You feel that others make decisions for you and that you cannot control your life. Or, you feel that you must control the thoughts, feelings, and actions of others.

You may have recognized yourself in one or more of the ten styles of distorted thinking. You will notice that you practice some styles more than others. Becoming familiar with all ten of the styles is useful. As you come to recognize them easily, you'll be in a better place to stop them before they can cause you real emotional pain. Complete the following exercises to get practice in distinguishing among the ten styles.

Exercise

Read the statements containing a cognitive fallacy. Write the number corresponding to the distortion in the blank space.

1. I must be just lazy.	_____	A. Filtering
2. I'll never get organized.	_____	B. Catastrophizing
3. If I don't get organized, I'll go crazy.	_____	C. Overgeneralization
4. They only want people who fit their mold.	_____	D. Labeling
5. I can tell he doesn't like me.	_____	E. Mind reading

6. She's so much better at
this than I am.   _____   F. Shoulds

7. Two Bs and a C. I'm failing here.   _____   G. Personalization

8. People should be more tolerant.   _____   H. Polarized thinking

9. If she really loved me,
she'd push me less.   _____   I. Fairness

10. I can't concentrate on this
work. I must be stupid.   _____   J. Control

Answers: 1-D, 2-B, 3-C, 4-J, 5-E, 6-G, 7-A, 8-F, 9-I, 10-H

Now try another set:

11. I'm unlovable.   _____   A. Filtering

12. She's thinking she doesn't
love me anymore.   _____   B. Catastrophizing

13. He should love me more
given all I do for him.   _____   C. Overgeneralization

14. Men only love sexy women.   _____   D. Labeling

15. She's so much more
lovable than I am.   _____   E. Mind Reading

16. In two dates he's only
mentioned marriage once.   _____   F. Shoulds

17. I'll never be loved.   _____   G. Personalization

18. If I'm not loved, I'll die.   _____   H. Polarization

19. I should be loved.   _____   I. Fairness

20. I can't get her attention
tonight. I must not be loved.   _____   J. Control

Answers: 11-A, 12-E, 13-I, 14-J, 15-G, 16-A, 17-B, 18-C, 19-F, 20-H.

Exercise

Try another exercise that is a little more difficult. Read the following examples and circle the distorted thinking style represented. There may be more than one.

1. Frank is a tough boss. He started out in sales and he was brilliant. The company promoted him to a management position so that he could teach the younger sales staff some of his techniques. Frank met with his new staff for the first time and gave them his pep talk.

   "I know you think you already know it all. There's nothing you can learn from an old coot like me. I'll tell you, though, you're nothing until you've stood the test of time in this business. You're just pups. It's rough out there. People won't let you get ahead. If you don't listen up, you'll never amount to anything."

   A. Overgeneralization   B. Labeling   C. Control

   D. Personalization   E. Shoulds   F. Mind reading

   Answers: F, C, B, A

2. Mary was in a panic. Her history and English literature exams were on Friday. She had put off preparing and was now losing a lot of sleep as she crammed each night. Mary thought, "How did I get in this mess? How could this happen to me? I should have been more careful. If only I hadn't spent so much time on my art project. I'm never going to get myself together. If I don't pass these exams, I'm going to flunk out and have no future. Why can't these professors be more understanding?"

   A. Filtering   B. Overgeneralization   C. Labeling

   D. Shoulds   E. Catastrophizing   F. Fairness

   Answers: D, B, E

3. Getting along with his in-laws was difficult for Morris. They saw him as lazy and felt he didn't keep their daughter in the comfort which they felt she deserved. Morris kept quiet for almost a year, but after their baby's baptism he really let his father-in-law have it. He said, "I can't stand it anymore. You're an overbearing jerk. I can tell you think I'm a loser. You think your daughter's the greatest thing that ever lived and I'm dirt. Either keep your feelings to yourself or something drastic will happen."

   A. Labeling   B. Polarized thinking   C. Catastrophizing

   D. Filtering   E. Mind reading   F. Personalization

   Answers: A, E, B

Rational Responses to Cognitive Distortions

The ten styles of cognitive distortions are irrational ways of thinking. This does not mean crazy ways of thinking—just emotionally based thinking. When these thoughts arouse fear and anger, you can find yourself highly involved with the feelings and not attending to the situation that generated them. Irrational thoughts create a compelling distraction. It's more immediately gratifying and stimulating to attend to intense emotion than to work through the situation that provoked it.

To combat this distortion, it's necessary to neutralize the emotions by rationally responding to these thoughts. The process involves identifying your distorted thought and then replacing it with a rational one. The following sections review the ten styles of distorted thinking and describe general strategies for replacing these thoughts.

Filtering

As a result of filtering, you have come to view the world as a frightening or hostile place. You are left feeling anxious or angry. To combat these troubling thoughts, your filter needs to be made less efficient. It needs to let other views of the world in. When you filter only a frightening thought, make an effort to think of a nonthreatening aspect of the experience, too. Remember Nigel, who only heard his boss's admonition to get the job done on time? He could also focus on the fact that his boss gave him two important assignments that morning and must have some trust in him. Similarly, search your present situation to find aspects that signify safety, plenty, or hope when you begin to overfocus on one negative experience. It's also helpful for you to identify your particular theme, such as, "I'm seeing this as a loss only." You can then better direct your thinking to a rational comeback based on a broader assessment of your current environment.

Catastrophizing

Catastrophic thinking can lead to paralysis. The fear of dire consequences is motivating only in life-and-death circumstances. To keep you from freezing with fear, it's necessary to think of other possible outcomes to the situation. Awareness that you are engaging in this type of thinking is a good guide to developing a comeback. Then think of at least one—or more, if you can—other outcome to the situation. If you fear that you will be hijacked on the highway when your car runs out of gas, think that someone you know will pass by, or that a police car will arrive. Generate as many noncatastrophic outcomes as you can.

Overgeneralization

Overgeneralization leads to false conclusions about your experiences and abilities. They are false because there is insufficient evidence to support your fear of always failing. To respond rationally to these misleading thoughts, ask yourself, "Where's the evidence?" Ask, "How do I know that for sure?" When your thinking is activated by asking questions, your rational side will overcome the emotionalism. Any evidence that you do produce should be questioned further. If you support your fear by saying, "The boss said so," ask yourself, "How does the boss know what my future will be?" How can your boss predict how you will perform in the future? If you keep a questioning mind, you will eventually expose your evidence as weak and insubstantial.

To avoid the overgeneralization trap, guard against using words such as *always, never,* and *everyone.* When you catch yourself exaggerating by using these words, stop and replace them with *sometimes, maybe,* and *someone.*

Labeling

Labeling involves reducing a person (or experience) to a single word. Even if it's positive, the label cannot do justice to the complexity of a person. When you find yourself labeling others, ask yourself what qualities this person has that are not included in this single label. Do not let yourself fall into the trap of only searching for further negative qualities that will substantiate your feelings. Actively look for positive or at least neutral aspects of this person. As you engage in this exercise, you will find your emotions cooling and a more rational balance returning.

To combat labeling, it's also effective to limit your label to a specific situation. If someone cuts you off at the stoplight, instead of saying, "What a jerk," you can be more specific in your criticism, such as, "What a jerky thing to do." Your anger will be more contained and less intense by imposing this rational perspective on your observation.

Mind Reading

Mind reading involves making snap decisions about how others think or feel. You are usually reading your own fears into the comments or expressions of others. To avoid this trap, it's best to be assertive and ask for clarification. Instead of assuming you know what others think, ask them. You can preface your question by saying, "I thought you might be feeling _____." Then ask if it is the case. Some situations do not permit such inquiries (for example, job interviews, or the classroom). At these times, it's a good idea to tolerate your confusion or fear. Tell yourself, though, that you are mind reading and really don't know what another person is thinking. Later you can evaluate the situation and closely examine what evidence you have to support your fears.

Shoulds

People are not all alike. Different experiences and cultures will lead to different values and rules about how things ought to be. To combat the mental fallacy about how people should behave, it's helpful to keep these differences in mind. When you make statements containing the words *should, ought,* or *must,* stop yourself and ask, "Why?" Why must people behave in a certain way? It might be good if they did, but why must they? Try replacing these imperatives with less aggravating words, such as *could,* or just wish for more socially adaptive behavior from others.

Personalization

Personalization has some similarity to mind reading. You assume that you know that others are thinking negatively of you. You go a step further and interpret all actions as being related to you. As a result, you feel that everything people do is a comment on you. Again, you are drawing a conclusion without adequate information. Combating this distorted style of thinking requires that you step back a little from the situation and acknowledge that those around you have an agenda of their own. Actively dissuade yourself from taking responsibility for others' feelings. Ask yourself for evidence that you are responsible.

Also resist the temptation to compare yourself to others. These comparisons may be habitual for you by now. As in breaking any bad habit, be aware that you are engaging in it; stop and replace it with a statement to yourself that you are a valuable person. Your worth does not depend on your ability to compete with others.

Polarized Thinking

Combating polarized thinking involves learning to see shades of gray. Instead of thinking in absolute terms, locate your experience on the continuum between the two poles (assign a specific percentage to your observations). Rose, for example, decided that her husband was selfish and incompetent after observing that he was preoccupied with a personal project. Rose could overcome her distorted style of thinking by remembering a number of generous acts her husband had made. She could then say, "He's selfish 25 percent of the time, but he's considerate 75 percent of the time." By clarifying her thinking, Rose can reduce her negative emotional arousal and then feel a lot less stress in her marriage.

Fairness

Feeling that life is unfair can lead to feelings of anger and rebellion. A person with ADD may have succumbed to these feelings from time to time. Many environments, such as school and work require sustained attention and orderliness—skills that the person with ADD find difficult to acquire and maintain. At the same time, with ADD, you most likely possess other talents that you feel you are not permitted to demonstrate in these structured environments. Feelings of unfairness may emerge.

Reducing the distraction of intense negative emotions requires reframing your experience of unfairness. Think of what you want as a preference instead of the right and fair way. Preferences then need to be communicated to others. When possible, let others know what you want. For example, let your spouse know you prefer to relax when you get home and then get your chores done. There are, of course, situations when you can't negotiate for what you want. In these events, a serene acceptance of the way things are is best.

Control

Combating the fallacy of control is an important step in overcoming the procrastination common for people with ADD. Feeling that your actions can make a difference is an effective motivation for taking on a new challenge. To avoid this cognitive trap, ask yourself for evidence that your efforts can't make a difference. How can you be sure that your efforts won't pay off? Along with this line of questioning, remind yourself that you make the decisions for *you*. How things turn out for you is the result of the choices you make. When the situation is not to your liking, you'll need to ask, "What can I do to change it?"

Rational Thinking

Taking control of your life is just the first step. Letting go of your responsibility for others is the next. Just as you are responsible for your decisions, others are responsible for theirs. This is not to say that you can't be supportive or helpful when asked, but that you permit others to have the freedom to succeed or fail for themselves.

Rational Responses to the Ten Fallacies of Thinking

Here is a summary of the ten cognitive distortions and how to combat them:

- Filtering: Identify your personal filter. Look for evidence contrary to filtered experience.
- Catastrophizing: Think of other, safe outcomes to your situation.
- Overgeneralization: Ask, "Where's the evidence?" Avoid using words such as *always, never, only,* and *everyone.*
- Labeling: Actively look for aspects of the person or situation that do not fit the label. Use labels to describe a specific situation only.
- Mind reading: Ask for clarification.
- Shoulds: Keep in mind that others have different experiences and may have different values. Replace "should" statements with "I want or wish" statements.
- Personalization: Let others be responsible for their feelings. Avoid comparing yourself to others.
- Polarized thinking: Learn to see shades of gray. And learn to be comfortable with these shades. Quantify your observations to put them in perspective.
- Fairness: Learn to see fairness as a preference for a way of acting.
- Control: Take responsibility for your choices. Let others be responsible for their decisions.

The Three-Column Technique

Aaron Beck describes a technique for combating distorted thinking. The technique uses three columns for identifying, labeling, and then replacing irrational statements like this:

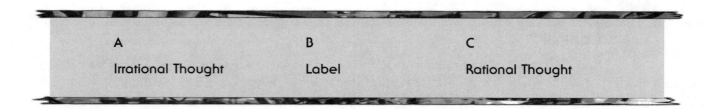

A	B	C
Irrational Thought	Label	Rational Thought

The structure of by the three-column technique provides a simple way of taking yourself through the process of replacing irrational statements with rational thoughts. Consider the following:

A	B	C
Irrational Thought	Label	Rational Thought
I'm always late.	Overgeneralization	I'm late this morning.
I'm lazy.	Labeling	Today I don't feel like mowing the lawn.
I'm going to lose it.	Catastrophizing	I'm upset but I can handle it.

Exercise

Now that you've practiced identifying and labeling emotional thoughts, the next step is to replace them with rational thoughts. Rewrite each of the following irrational thoughts in rational terms.

1. I know you think you already know it all. _____

_____

2. People won't let me get ahead. _____

_____

3. I should have been more careful. _____

_____

4. I'm never going to get myself together. _____

_____

5. You're an overbearing jerk. _____

_____

6. I'm a loser. _____

_____

Until you are very experienced at the replacement process, it will be too cumbersome to try to analyze and replace thoughts as they happen. With practice, you'll be able to identify and replace distorted, depressing thoughts quickly and easily. This practice will give you enormous relief from the self-defeating thoughts you previously endured.

Exercise

Use the three-column technique to guide your practice in rational thinking. You will need to practice on a daily basis for several weeks. In your early stage of combating distortions, set aside a time each day to remember difficult, emotion-provoking situations. Use the form on the following page to structure your daily practice.

Summary

- Depression, a common problem for adults with ADD, can be treated with both medication and behavior therapy.

- One theory of behavior therapy states that how you interpret events affects the way you feel about them, and negative interpretation of experiences often happens without your realizing it. You base many interpretations on automatic thoughts, which distort your experience.

- Ten common automatic thoughts—called cognitive distortions—have been identified: filtering, catastrophizing, overgeneralization, labeling, mind reading, shoulds, personalization, polarized thinking, fairness, and control.

- Combating distortions requires neutralizing emotions by responding rationally to these thoughts. Another technique, called the three-column technique, uses a process of identifying, labeling, and replacing distorted thoughts with emotionally calm, rational thoughts.

Combating Distortions

Day _____   Date _____

A	B	C
Irrational Thought	Label	Rational Thought
1. _____	_____	_____
_____	_____	_____
2. _____	_____	_____
_____	_____	_____
3. _____	_____	_____
_____	_____	_____
4. _____	_____	_____
_____	_____	_____
5. _____	_____	_____
_____	_____	_____
6. _____	_____	_____
_____	_____	_____

Rational Thinking

6

Focusing:

Plan, Structure, and Persevere in Your Task

With ADD you have the special ability to hyperfocus when circumstances are right. But it's more often the case that getting down to business is a difficult task.

> Linda is a 24-year-old, first-year graduate student in art history. Her ADD was diagnosed in high school after her college placement scores indicated that she was much more capable than her C grade point average suggested. Linda is disorganized. Her room is a mess. She loses things frequently and spends valuable time looking for misplaced items. She is a dreamer and seems to lose track of time. Deadlines approach and she is constantly caught unaware. She has to scramble to keep up and never produces work she thinks is her best. Living with a sense of chaos leaves her feeling discouraged. She feels she can't get organized, get started, or finish what she wants.

Procrastination is a common complaint among adults with ADD. Recent research has linked procrastination to "low-conscientiousness," suggesting an ADD profile for one type of procrastination. Characteristics include poor attention to detail, difficulty concentrating, restlessness, and difficulty with planning and follow-through. Learning to effectively focus your energy—to stop procrastinating—will be a major accomplishment. It's likely that you have a history of trying to get organized but have found no system that works for long. You may have worked hard to get your desk cleaned on Monday only to find it buried again by Friday. Succeeding will require flexibility on your part and a willingness to experiment.

This chapter and the next one provide a system for starting and finishing a task. The key element is structure. You will need to structure your time, environment, and thoughts about getting things done. Studies show that instruction in time management alone has not been effective in overcoming procrastination. Simply organizing work and time does not get the job done, although it's a necessary first step. Getting started and working through to the finish also require managing distractions, negative feelings, and thoughts about your work. Throughout this chapter and the next, you will engage in self-assessment exercises and learn to plan, structure, and persevere. Select one task that you've been avoiding lately to use in the exercises. Choose a project that has some immediate importance to you but not one that is critical. Make this a practice problem—one that you can experiment with. Try out the techniques and practice until you have worked out a plan that suits you and gets the job done.

Exercise

Write down the task that you have been avoiding and will work on for the next two chapters.

_____

_____

_____

Excuses—Fuel for Procrastination

Excuses provide the means—a rationale—for escaping the difficulty of the present. It's clear from the research on procrastination that excuse making is highly correlated with putting things off. Excuses can occur at any time and derail a project that has finally gotten under way. Excuses come in many varieties. Some are subtle and most have a kernel of truth. But their purpose is to stop your long-range plans and provide short-term gratification. Awareness of the excuses you make—calling them by name—is the first step in avoiding their trap.

Needing Inspiration

People with ADD often are creative or inventive. Ideas can flood the mind—sometimes all at once (or so it seems). At other times, though, your mind comes to a dead stop. It's tempting to say, at these times, that you're not in the mood to work. You want to wait for inspiration to strike. In assuming you need to feel motivated to go on, you're giving yourself an out—an excuse—for quitting. Work, creative endeavors, or just routine tasks, do _not_ need inspiration to be completed. A highly charged mood is a bonus but not a necessity for getting

1. Do I sometimes blame others for the state that I'm in? Yes _____ No _____

2. Do I sometimes get caught up with negative emotions and feel I can't focus on work?
    Yes _____ No _____

3. Do I find myself waiting, thinking that someone else will finish for me? Yes _____
    No _____

things done. Ernest Hemingway, who displayed many characteristics of ADD (frequent job/career changes, substance abuse, moodiness, unstable relationships) was also a prolific writer. He attributed his success not to inspiration but to sitting himself down for four hours every morning and working at his craft.

Waiting

Not feeling ready to persist often leads to a promise to get it done tomorrow—or some later date. The problem with waiting is that tomorrow always has its own demands, and yesterday's work will be forgotten. It would be the rare case when tomorrow really is a better time to finish than today. Related to postponing until another time, is waiting for some intermediary event to occur. For example, some people feel that they cannot quit smoking until they have lost a few extra pounds because without cigarettes they will eat even more and compound a weight problem. It can be difficult to quit smoking and to lose weight, but both are important and are independent of the other.

Blaming

Blaming others is a way of distracting yourself from what you really want to do. If you feel that others (parents, teachers, coaches, and so on) have not prepared you for the challenges of your life, you can avoid feeling responsible for what you do. It can be easy to give up or not even try when you feel let down by others around you.

Emotionalism

Blaming others usually leads to feelings of resentment and even anger. These emotions and others can powerfully command your attention and distract you from a task at hand. Emotions, especially strong ones, are immediate and require our present energy to manage them. It's easy to tell yourself that you are just too upset to get down to the mundane, day-to-day tasks or push ahead toward your goal. It takes practice and awareness to keep emotions separated from the work you need to do.

Being Rescued

When the work gets difficult or boring, it's tempting to slow down or quit altogether. You may have had this experience and found that someone jumped in for you and completed the project. Parents often find it easier to pick up after children, or even to finish their homework for them, than to nag the child to completion. When you've been rescued in the past, it's tempting to sit back and hope that this technique will work again. Rescue is likely to occur in the workplace when deadlines are real and projects must be completed. Often a co-worker or subordinate will be assigned the job of finishing the task. Of course, failure to follow through may jeopardize a promotion or even continued employment.

Exercise

Think of the task you have been avoiding that you wrote down at the beginning of this chapter. What excuses have you used for not getting started?

Elements of Organization

Labeling your behavior is instructive and puts a break in the action. You can then go on to substitute more effective, task-focused techniques for getting things done. Developing and sustaining your focus will be a major accomplishment. It's likely that you have a history of trying to get organized but have found that no system works for long. There is no simple solution. And there is no one right way to approach organizing time and tasks. You will need to experiment and to find your own style.

Structuring and directing your energy is a complex skill. It's made up of planning, organizing, and managing aspects of work and behavior. Awareness of your behavior style and alertness to possible obstacles also is needed. It can take time and practice to get all of these skills going together. When you combine these skills with skills to maintain focus until the task is finished, you will have acquired the "master" skill of self-management.

The rest of the chapter outlines a number of common components for organizing time and getting started on tasks. Taken together, the techniques provide a complete system for selecting jobs, organizing and finding the time to do them.

Lists

Lists are the first step in creating structure for your work. Lists serve many purposes. The first is to clarify thinking. In the act of making a list, ideas are refined and rejected. Putting a task on paper also serves to heighten its importance and to increase your commitment. Once completed, the list serves as a memory jogger. There are, however, a number of fine points to this simple idea.

First, it is a good idea to have a list for each important area of your life. Keep a list of things to do at work and a separate one for tasks at home. A list of personal or self-care tasks is also useful, but keep the number of lists to a minimum. Too many lists are confusing, and the sense of so many things to be done will seem overwhelming.

Some people report anxiety in making a list. They worry that they have forgotten something. Others agonize over whether to include some task. When making the list, jot down what you think is relevant and then go on. You can always revise the list later. If you find you are still struggling over making the list, set a time limit. Give yourself five minutes, and then move on to other things. Use a kitchen timer, if needed.

Once made, a list can be easily forgotten. To make the list useful, you need to have it handy and to refer to it often. Post your list in a prominent place. The refrigerator is typically a good spot, since most people use it frequently. At work, post the list on your lamp or bulletin board. Use color coding—a bright red or yellow paper for your list can make it stand out from a lot of other, white paper.

Your list can be written on a small piece of paper that you carry with you. Or you may find it more effective to write each task on a separate sheet of full-size paper. Then place the papers—in order of priority—above your desk at work or in some conspicuous place at home. You can reorder your priorities by rearranging the sheets. Making the list large helps to keep your tasks in view, giving a visual reminder of what to do. A simple to-do list is shown on the next page.

You will need to decide on a time frame for your list. Making a list and then carrying it around day to day, week to week will not be very helpful. Daily lists are useful, and revising them each day also serves as feedback on how you are keeping up with the work to be done. You may find that weekly lists more naturally fit the task, such as grocery shopping or other housework.

Finally, date the list when it's made and include an expiration date. When the list expires, spend a minute reviewing the list. Think of what you have accomplished and be sure to congratulate yourself. Look, too, at what remains to be done. Honestly evaluate why tasks remain. Then, decide if they are still important and, if so, include them on the next list.

Deadlines

To help avoid a lot of excuse making, such as, "I'll do it tomorrow," set a deadline for completing your job. Like making lists, setting a deadline helps to clarify thinking. You'll necessarily think about when the work needs to be done. To set a realistic deadline, also consider what other events are occurring in your life. Take into account the time you will need for holidays and special projects as well as just day-to-day events.

It helps to set a deadline with some time to spare. This extra time can be used to polish the work or to make up time if setbacks have occurred. However, for people with ADD, a bit of pressure nearing the deadline can be a good thing. Too much extra time will usually just lead to distractions, and the pressure of cutting it close can help heighten attention and increase concentration.

Schedules

When your lists are made and your deadline set, you have a clearer sense of what you want to do. It's time then to think concretely about how all this work will get done. This chapter provides suggestions and schedule forms for a week's planning. A weekly schedule is not so shortsighted as one day at a time but not as overwhelming as a month. For your

Exercise

Practice making lists of things to do. Copy the form below and use it to make lists for important aspects of your life.

To-Do List

Task _____

Date _____   Expiration _____

1. _____
2. _____
3. _____
4. _____
5. _____
6. _____
7. _____
8. _____
9. _____
10. _____

business or school work, it may be necessary to plan on a six-month or semester basis. Other tasks, such as planning a long trip, may take a month. It's best if you experiment and find your own comfortable time frame for planning your work.

It's important to set a specific day and time at the beginning of each week to fill in the schedule. After you practice scheduling for a few weeks, you will find that it gets easier and eventually becomes a habit. You'll naturally use this time each week to get organized.

When using a weekly schedule, set aside a time each day to review the plans for that day. This is the time to revise your schedule, glance over the tasks, and make a commitment to getting things done.

To complete a schedule (a sample that you can copy and use is shown on the following page), first fill in all the standing, necessary tasks, such as driving to work, eating, fixing dinner, picking up children from school. Then, using the lists you have made, schedule time for those projects. Last, but definitely not least, fill in time for yourself. People with ADD often need time each day just to let the mental wheels spin. Time for relaxation, special projects, and just doing nothing is essential for mental rejuvenation.

Remember to be useful, a schedule must be handy. Make a few copies and post them at work, home, or in your car, and carry one with you in your pocket, purse, or briefcase. You can make individual tasks more prominent, too, by using markers for color coding. For example, make your most critical tasks each day stand out by coloring them red. Use other colors to create visual interest or to signal important work.

A technique that works well for some is to exchange schedules with a friend. Then make it a point to talk over your schedules together. You can provide encouragement, suggestions, and feedback for each other.

Taking Small Steps

People with ADD often have big ideas. They can be truly visionary. The problem comes when the vision has to be made real. The amount of work involved seems overwhelming, and nothing gets done. Criticism for lack of follow-through often results. When your task is a dream or just the necessity of painting the house, it can seem overwhelming. The solution is to break the larger task down into its smaller steps. Each smaller task can seem more manageable, and progress can begin. If the smaller tasks still seem overwhelming, break them down into even smaller steps. This process of breaking down a larger task into its smaller components can continue until you are comfortable working on each step. The list of subtasks in a large job also serves as a checklist for completing the job. Check off each small step as you go and give yourself feedback on your progress. The checklist further serves as a memory jog, so that you don't forget—or have to worry about forgetting—small but essential steps in your progress.

Pacing Yourself

The success of your schedule will depend to a great degree on how accurately you are able to estimate the time required for each task. If you greatly underestimate the time needed, you are going to feel pressured and wonder whether you can really manage your time at all. If you grossly overestimate the time needed, you leave yourself open to distractions.

To estimate the time needed for any job, you'll need to practice making estimates. Usually, when estimating time, you'll think of your total project and then guess. A better way

Exercise

Complete the following schedule with all required activities for the week. Include time to commute, work, and so on. Fill in time on the schedule to work on your task.

	Monday	Tuesday	Wednesday	Thursday	Friday	Saturday	Sunday
7 am							
8 am							
9 am							
10 am							
11 am							
Noon							
1 pm							
2 pm							
3 pm							
4 pm							
5 pm							
6 pm							
7 pm							
8 pm							
9 pm							
10 pm							

Exercise

Using the form below, take an item from your to-do list and break it down into smaller steps. Ignore the "Estimated Time to Complete" and "Time Actually Required" columns for now. They will be explained in a later section.

List of Subtasks

	Check When Done	Subtask	Estimated Time to Complete	Time Actually Required
1.	☐	_____	_____	_____
2.	☐	_____	_____	_____
3	☐	_____	_____	_____
4.	☐	_____	_____	_____
5.	☐	_____	_____	_____
6.	☐	_____	_____	_____
7.	☐	_____	_____	_____
8.	☐	_____	_____	_____
9.	☐	_____	_____	_____
10.	☐	_____	_____	_____

Total Time: ___   Total Time: ___

is to break the task down into all of its smaller steps, and then estimate how long you will need at each step. Your estimate will be much more accurate. Then add up the time required for your total job.

When estimating time for each smaller step of the job, compare it to some similar task you have successfully completed in the past. Use this past experience as your first estimate. If you have no similar experience or just want another opinion, ask other people how long it would take them to complete that step. Keep your lists, small steps, and time estimates in separate folders. Together they will form a database for future projects. Once you have estimated the time needed for a task or subtask, use this information to schedule your time.

Exercise

Using the form on the previous page, estimate the time each small step will require and fill it in under "Estimated Time to Complete."

Making Transitions

Most people find it difficult to transition from one task to another. Adults with ADD find it all too easy to switch from task to task. These abrupt changes in direction leave some tasks stalled and others rushed. Jumping from one task to another usually creates a disjointed product, since loose ends are not attended to.

Successful transitioning takes practice and determination. To develop this skill, set a specific time that you will stop working on your task. Set a kitchen or watch timer to signal you when your time is up; then *stop*. Give yourself a few minutes break, and then begin the next task. Again, set your timer to signal the time to stop. Initially you may find yourself restless and feeling ineffective when starting a new task. These feelings and the accompanying thoughts often give you a reason to stop. Feeling ineffective isn't much of a motivation to continue. But it's important to persist in spite of these feelings. You will find yourself gradually warming up to the task and getting focused if you persist. As with any skill, the more you practice, the easier it will become.

1. Do I find it difficult to stop a task that I am involved in? Yes _____ No _____

2. Do I need a great deal of time to stop one task and then start another? Yes _____ No _____

Summary

- Excuse making is highly correlated with procrastination—a common problem for adults with ADD. Common excuses include waiting for inspiration, planning to do it later, blaming others, being emotional, and being rescued.

- Focusing on a task requires setting up a structure for getting things done. Some techniques that help create structure are

    Creating lists

    Setting deadlines

    Making schedules

    Breaking tasks down into smaller steps

- Adults with ADD find it difficult to start and stop working on a task as needed. Learning to estimate the amount of time a job will take, setting a timer, and practicing transitions can help to develop these skills.

7

Finishing:

Reap the Rewards

Planning, organizing, and scheduling provide essential structure to get the job started. But additional techniques are needed to bring it to completion.

Rob, a high-powered sales manager for a biotech company has a problem finishing most things. His house is littered with magazines that are half read. He keeps them around, thinking that he'll get back to them someday. He has a more serious problem at work—finishing deals that he's started. Rob enjoys the initial stage of a new sales campaign. He's good at staking out a territory and carefully pursuing clients. But as soon as the deal seems sure, he's lost interest. He starts thinking about the next new project—learning to scuba dive, or building an addition on the house. His support staff have saved him many times, but Rob has lost more than one account because of his difficulty in following through.

Gary, too, has problems bringing a job to its conclusion. He's a housepainter and loves his work. He likes the immediate feedback of transforming the old into the new. Gary has problems when it comes to cleaning up at the end of the day. His problem stems from his inability to define cleanup as part of the job. He feels that when the painting is over, he's done. Gary infuriates his customers with his lack of follow-through. He's lucky that he's so good at his work.

Losing interest in a task is a common problem for people with ADD. Maintaining attention after the novelty has worn off is a struggle, and losing this battle leads to many abandoned projects. Losing interest also leaves you open to distractions. Distractions, which are more immediately stimulating than your current work, seem irresistible. Other obstacles can also derail a good start. Not planning for each step of the project, right through to the finish, can leave you without needed structure when energy and attention run low. This chapter will look at common problems that derail the best-laid plans. It contains suggestions and exercises to help you surmount them and take your work to its final step, and reap *all* the rewards.

1. Do I often get to the end of my work and find aspects that I had not considered? Yes _____ No _____

2. Do I end up with less than I had hoped because I had to "wing it" at the end? Yes _____ No _____

3. Am I often scrambling at the end of a task to complete parts I had not thought of or planned for initially? Yes _____ No _____

Plan to the Finish

Gary receives a lot of immediate feedback from his work as a housepainter. Seeing results before his eyes keeps him going throughout long workdays. But he doesn't define the final stage of work—cleanup—as part of the job. He does not think the job all the way through. To his customers, cleanup is almost as important as the painting itself. Gary needs to plan how to complete each step of the job. Leaving out the last step of your work is annoying to others. It can be devastating to your success if you don't thoroughly plan projects, whether they are painting a house, negotiating a contract, or moving to a new apartment.

It's not easy to see all the way to the end of a project from the beginning, especially if the task is new to you or the work is difficult, tedious, or lengthy. In a situation like this, it's very useful to have a task partner. You may be good at dreaming up the idea, but you may need someone who is logical and works sequentially to take it to the final step.

Although teamwork can be a problem for people with ADD, you'll find you need a steady eye to guide you through. If you can't work with a partner, at least get feedback from others about your plan. Be active. Ask questions. Ask others if they can see problems and suggest solutions. Thinking your own way through to the end is important. Watch how your partners plan each step and take note of their techniques. You also can use your powers of visualization to imagine the final step of your work. Be very complete in your thinking. Imagine what you will have, how it will look, and how you will feel at the end of your work.

Exercise

Think about the task you chose to work on in chapter 6, and describe how you will determine that you have thought your task through to the end. List the techniques you will use. Here are two examples to give you the idea:

Task: fix the kitchen door

Will be complete when: door closes easily, floor is swept, tools back in garage

Techniques I will use: work with son, Jake. Assign him sweeping job

Task: make date for Saturday

Will be complete when: I have set time to meet, I have picked up tickets

Techniques I will use: Ask Ben to go with me to pick up tickets

Managing Distractions

Distractibility is one of the distinguishing features of ADD. Your mind can wander off in many fascinating directions and lead to very inventive ideas. But, when the job requires moving directly from point A to point B, distractions are a disaster. Distractions come in different forms, though, and once you distinguish among expected and unexpected distractions, you can apply different techniques in dealing with them.

Expected Distractions

Most distractions that derail good intentions are not really out of the blue. Instead, these distractions are ordinary events that you can reasonably predict, such as hearing the mail drop through the slot at 2:30 p.m. or suddenly becoming aware of the ticking desk clock. Ordinary sounds can be distracting to the person with ADD, whose brain is constantly on the lookout for stimulation. Other examples of expected distractions include the kids asking for snacks when they come home from school or the office gossip dropping in after the weekly staff meeting.

Another type of expected distraction comes from within. This distraction includes those inner urges to take a break—to raid the refrigerator, make a phone call, or just sharpen your pencil when the task gets boring. These inner urges may not seem expected at that moment, but if you honestly reflect on your work habits, you know you often go offtrack when these ideas strike.

Organization

Structuring your environment is the first, best step to take in managing distractions. It's important to choose where you work so that you can maximize concentration and minimize distractions. Your place of work should be comfortable for *you*. If you feel cramped or claustrophobic, or conversely, if your work space is too big and it echoes, it's a distraction, and you'll find you want to avoid this place. You should be able to move around a bit and get into and out of the area easily. Be sure there is good ventilation and lighting, too. You'll become fatigued if you're straining your eyes or not getting enough fresh air.

Eliminate all known distractions. For example, if you work at home, don't locate your work space near the refrigerator if you're tempted by food. Also, don't work facing the TV. People with ADD often find that some sort of sound can aid concentration by blocking out random noise, but the TV tends to be too variable in the sounds it produces, and there's always the temptation to *look* at the set as well. Listening to music can boost concentration. Some ADDers even work better when listening to loud rock music.

Depending on your work, you may find that you need the telephone close at hand. Problems can occur when the phone is used as a distraction. The tedium of some tasks can be particularly difficult for someone with ADD. You may have the impulsive urge to pick up the phone and create some interest. If the phone is a distraction, place it out of your work space. You will then need to move to the phone to use it in a planned, constructive way. Create a list of people to call while you're working. Then set aside a specific time to go through the list to decide first, if the call is necessary, then the best time to call.

Exercise

Use the following questions to evaluate your work space.

1. Where do I choose to do my work that requires concentration (home, office, school)? And how does the setting affect my ability to concentrate? _____

_____

_____

2. Do I feel physically comfortable in this setting? _____

Why? _____

Why not? _____

3. Am I interrupted or distracted frequently? _____

What are the distractions? _____

_____

It's also very important to use you work space for work only. If you are consistent in working in this space and *no* other, the space will come to signal *work* automatically. You'll gradually have an easier time of concentrating in this space.

Exercise

Evaluate your work space for heating, lighting, space, distractions.

Problems

1. _____

2. _____

3. _____

4. _____

5. _____

Solutions

1. _____

2. _____

3. _____

4. _____

5. _____

Reminders

Another technique for keeping yourself alert to distractions is to post signs in your work environment. If your eyes pass over a note on your computer screen saying "Stay Focused" or "Keep Thinking," you're more likely to catch yourself drifting off before you've gone on a thirty-minute tangent. If these signs would not be acceptable in your workplace, use some other signal, such as a red dot, in a prominent place to remind you to stay focused. Depending on where you work, you may be able to post signs outside your door area to let others know that you're busy and can't be disturbed. It's helpful if you include on your "do not disturb" signs when you will be available for interruptions.

The inner urges that seem so compelling at the time also need your management. If you find you are distracted by hunger, thirst, or the need to use the bathroom, plan your work time to incorporate scheduled breaks. As described in chapter 6, set a time limit and then return to your task. When the inner urge is for novelty or stimulation, you must recognize your distraction. It's best to clearly label it, "I'm being distracted." Often this simple, self-observation is enough for you to overcome the urge and return to work. When the urge is strong, though, you'll need some mental techniques to successfully fight it off. At this time, it's useful to have a clear sense of why you need to concentrate *now*. For this purpose jot down a few important points about your work and keep the list handy or post it in front of your nose. You may need to remind yourself that the test is tomorrow, or that you're already two weeks late with the report for your boss. Repeating these motivating statements to yourself a few times will help to successfully stifle the urge to escape the present. For longer term projects such as writing a thesis, remodeling the laundry room, or revising your photography portfolio, you can generate a list of positive outcomes for completing your job.

Exercise

For the task you're working on, list your reasons to get it done now.

1. _____

2. _____

3. _____

4. _____

5. _____

Unexpected Distractions

Not all distractions can be avoided. At times, the world will break through your concentration no matter how carefully you have selected your workplace, time, or prepared yourself with a rationale. Unexpected distractions do occur, such as loud, sudden noises, visitors, or telephone calls. Your first task is to assess the importance of the distraction. If it's your boss on the line, you will most likely accept the call and deal with the distraction. But if it's your tennis partner calling to set a date to play, you need to be able to resist the temptation to escape your work at that time. If you are reading up on the latest stereo technology for a course you're taking and stumble onto a solution to programming your CD player, you don't need to succumb to the urge to try it out now. Keep a notebook handy so that you can briefly write down these sudden ideas.

Task-Directed Thinking

Distractions are a major obstacle to getting things done for people with ADD. However, your ADD can also be why you lose interest in a project, especially if the initial, novel stage of the work has passed. Remember Rob, who was able to focus when the chase was on, but as soon as the deal seemed sure, his mind wandered off to more novel activities? People with ADD seek stimulation—they seem to need and thrive on new and interesting ideas. But, of course, plodding along to the finish is also needed for success. Another obstacle to finishing work is becoming overwhelmed by the task as the work progresses. Sometimes it's not easy to gauge the length or difficulty of work at the outset. We all try to make good guesses, but there can be unforeseen complications. The frustration you feel when the task gets really hard can lead to work slowdowns, and it's at this time that you are particularly susceptible to distractions.

When loss of interest or fatigue sets in, you'll need a technique for combating the urge to abandon your task. The urge to quit can occur at any time or place, so it's best that your strategy not be tied to any specific environment. Remembering your initial reasons for pursuing the task is effective here. Make a list of reasons to complete your job. List the benefits of completing your task on one sheet. On another, list the negative consequences of not finishing. Then post these lists where you will see them. You may need several locations for your lists: your office, inside your medicine cabinet, on the refrigerator, for example. Also write them on index cards and carry them in your datebook. Whenever you use your schedule, you'll be reminded of your reasons and you'll persevere.

Exercise

List the benefits of getting your job done:

1. _____

2. _____

3. _____

4. _____

5. _____

List the negative consequences for you of not getting your job done:

1. _____

2. _____

3. _____

4. _____

5. _____

Finishing

Rewarding Yourself

With ADD you often experience a letdown at the end of a major piece of work. Others may be celebrating around you, but you're feeling flat. You have spent a lot of energy keeping your focus over the period of time. The effort needed to concentrate, combat distractions, and remain alert can be pretty draining. The problem with this post-project letdown is that you aren't enjoying the experience of success. Rewarding yourself for a job well done or just for hanging in until the end is an important part of the work process. Rewards are meant to be enticing—to motivate you and even inspire you to engage in difficult work again. Skipping the reward experience will weaken your work habits.

As an ADDer, it sometimes feels as if you are a round peg living in a square world. "Do it this way," "Have it in by Friday," "Why haven't you done . . . ?" are comments thrown at you. The world is judged by the squares, so your contributions to the work as it progresses can seem to be marked down, belittled, or just plain stolen. Remember, the sequence is

$$idea \longrightarrow produce \longrightarrow reward$$

Master the techniques to do all three, all the way to finish line. That way *you* will collect the reward at the end.

Rewards do not need to be grand to be effective. You may decide to take off for a hiking expedition through the Rocky Mountains once you finally complete cleaning the garage or formulating a business plan. But something smaller can be just as effective—dinner out or time to listen to music is a reward, too. David Premack discovered in 1963 that letting someone engage in a higher probability behavior could be used to increase the occurrence of a lower probability behavior. That is, notice what you do a lot of (high-probability behavior), and you can use that activity for increasing the amount of something you're not likely to do (low-probability behavior). Teachers have been using this technique for centuries by scheduling a recess to follow a difficult lesson.

It's also important not to save all of the goodies for the end of your job. If you can wait until you've painted the entire house or completed graduate school to partake of rewards,

1. Do I find myself losing interest in my work after the initial excitement of the idea passes? Yes _____ No _____

2. Do I sometimes have difficulty estimating how hard a job may be? Yes _____ No _____

3. When the job is harder than I thought, do I feel a great deal of frustration? Yes _____ No _____

4. When the frustration builds up, do I get distracted by easier work? Yes _____ No _____

you'll feel pretty down (that is, if you can really keep going through all that deprivation). Schedule rewards to occur at natural breaks in your work. Using the small steps approach to big tasks, you can schedule some kind of reward at the end of each small amount of work completed.

Rewards are important for everyone, but for people with ADD, they're critical. Rewards provide a break in the monotony of work, add spark and stimulation to the day. With ADD you have a compressed experience of time; long stretches of work are difficult to tolerate. Smaller but more frequent rewards bridge the stages from start to finish of difficult tasks.

What rewards will I enjoy for completing my work?

_____

_____

_____

_____

Summary

- It's as important to manage the internal states of boredom, physical discomfort, and fatigue as the selection of time and place that you work. A breakdown in this process at any point will result in an incomplete effort. To complete work, think it through to its final steps. If possible, work with someone who is methodical, and get feedback from others about your plans. Develop visual skills to see your work at its end point.

- Make your work area comfortable. Be sure to have good lighting, ventilation, and enough room to move around in. Steer clear of distractions (TV, refrigerator, phone), and consider using music to block out noise.

- Recognize distractions—both expected and unexpected—when they occur. To combat them, make lists of reasons to finish your work, use reminders to return your focus to your work.

- Plan to reward yourself after completing each step of your work. Rewards do not need to be large or expensive. You can use any activity that you like doing as a reward.

8

Mood Management:

Techniques for Balancing the Highs and Lows

Janet has her own studio after leaving a dozen jobs in ten years. She feels free now "to be herself." "Herself," though, can seem unpredictable to others. Janet sometimes wakes up in a bad mood. Irritability may continue throughout the day or wear off gradually. She, as well as her friends, never knows what to expect. She can have a pretty good day and suddenly begin to feel blue. She gets tired easily, especially after concentrating on a long photo shoot, but that doesn't really explain the depth of her blues. Small slights from others can send her reeling. She may brood for days over a minor misunderstanding. Her friends tell her to "lighten up" or "get over it." She would if she could. Other times the bad feelings seem to come out of nowhere. She tries to shake them off, but they persist. Janet used alcohol in the past but kicked that habit. She also saw a psychiatrist once and tried an antidepressant. But so far, nothing has worked for long.

Just as your ability to concentrate and sit still will vary day to day, so will your moods and your ability to cope with your feelings. Irritability, depression, and swings from excited highs to gloomy lows are common. You may experience mood shifts that are tied to events, such as long periods of concentration or the letdown after a task is completed. Other shifts may be related to minor events, or have no explanation at all. Your response to experience is likely to be strong. ADDers typically overreact to emotional events and are often called "intense" or "thin-skinned" by others. A lot of the emotional ups and downs for ADDers results from the intense orientation to the external environment. When the boss is happy, you feel up. When your spouse is cross, you are down. People with ADD have trouble setting up barriers between themselves and the world. An ADDer can feel like an emotional slave.

As difficult as mood swings and emotional overreaction may be, ADDers are often reluctant to learn new ways of coping. Many people with ADD believe that stress is necessary for them to focus and tackle most tasks. There's some truth to this notion. With ADD you do need some heightened stimulation to get started. But there are ways to regulate your emotional reaction to events. You can learn to relax and feel in control. The highs and lows of this everyday experience can be exasperating and exhausting. Friends, family, and co-workers suffer, too. They never know what to expect and feel bewildered when your moods change quickly. Understanding and managing your moods are critical skills for success in every aspect of your life.

Becoming Aware of Your Moods

Before moods can be changed or even managed, you must be aware of the feelings that you have. If you are used to daily experiences of highs and lows, you may take mood shifts for granted and not notice when they occur. Before starting any intervention, do some daily mood monitoring. You'll get a sense of the intensity and frequency of your mood shifts. With this information, you will know where to concentrate your efforts and be able to measure your progress.

Exercise

Copy the form on the following page and use it daily to monitor your moods. Several times each day, stop and take note of your mood. Write the time. Do not label "good" or "bad" in the Feelings column. Name the mood (feeling), for example, irritable, happy, angry, or sad. Rate the intensity of your mood from 1 (not intense at all) to 10 (as intense as it can get for you.) Then it's important to notice what you were doing and thinking at the time. Finally, identify who was present when the mood struck. This information will help you to identify patterns—time of day, tasks, and so on—that may influence your feelings.

Anticipating Your Moods

With the information from your mood monitor, you will be able to better anticipate your moods. You may note, for example, that your irritability builds as the weekend approaches and you know your spouse is going to nag you to paint the shutters; or you may find that mornings are your most difficult time. Some moods that are atypical for most people are common for ADDers. For example, people with ADD often feel anxious when things are going well. This anxiety can be bewildering and frustrating for friends and family. Just as they want

Mood Monitor

Day _____   Date _____

Time	Feelings	Intensity (1-10)	Activity and People Present

to relax and enjoy success, you may suddenly get uptight and annoyed. As an adult with ADD, you may find it hard to relax, thinking that if you do, you'll start to lose your focus, you'll forget something, and mess up again.

It's also common with ADD to feel let down, even depressed, after a successful effort. Again, others want to celebrate, but you feel blue. This letdown may be caused by exhaustion because it takes more effort for you to see projects through to completion. As a result, you may feel let down or "wiped out" for a while.

Exercise

Once you have become familiar with identifying your moods, you're ready to do something to manage them. Below you will find five techniques for keeping yourself on an even keel. For any given mood, you may use two or three techniques—or you may need all five.

1. Label your mood. Just by identifying it, you'll take some steam out of the highs and alleviate the lows.

   What mood am I feeling right now? _____

2. Have a standard response ready; for example, "There's that old anxiety again" or "I expected this letdown. I know it will pass." These statements make the mood seem familiar—no big deal. They are comforting.

   What statement can I say to myself over and over to help me feel in control? _____

   _____

3. Have a plan. When you feel down, have a few uplifting videos to watch, friends to call, or good books to read.

   What will I do next time I feel down? Who will I call? _____

   What's a good movie to watch? Book to read? Music to listen to? _____

4. Save some time each day just to do nothing. Often ADDers need time at the end of the day to unwind—to let the wheels spin. It may be the only way your mind can slow down.

   Do I need some downtime each day? _____

   When can I have this time to myself? _____

   How much time do I need? _____

5. When you feel that you are being overwhelmed, take a break. A brief time-out from stimulation may be all you need to get on an even keel again.

   Where can I go at home to take a break? _____

   Where can I go at work? _____

Managing Mood Shifts

Now that you've identified some of your problem moods and learned how to anticipate them, you will want to try some techniques for getting them under control. Deep breathing, visualization, exercise, music, laughter, and good sleep are all natural ways to reduce stress and improve emotional stability. These techniques also require no special equipment and cost little or no money. They are portable and can be used in any environment. It's useful to develop your skills in as many of these areas as you can. Moods will continue to vary day to day; thus, it is important to remain flexible and vary your mood-management strategy as needed.

What Could I Possibly Need to Know About Breathing?

Breathing is the most natural act that you perform. It is automatic and practiced every minute of every day. What could you possibly need to know about breathing? To start with, knowing what happens to your body when you breathe and how different ways of breathing affect your well-being will help you learn to use breathing as a way to relax and stabilize your moods.

The diaphragm is a sheet-like muscle located at the base of the ribcage. It expands and contracts as you breathe in and out. When contracting, the diaphragm pushes air through the lungs. Blood pumped through the lungs by the heart is oxygenated during the breathing process. Oxygen-rich blood is bright red and provides nourishment to cells throughout the body. As blood passes through arteries and capillaries, the oxygen is released and the blood turns a dark, dull red color. Blood is pumped through the lungs, where it is deoxygenated and circulated again to the entire body. When this essential natural process is diminished by insufficient fresh air to your lungs, your organs and tissues do not obtain sufficient oxygen. Over time, this insufficiency will tire your system and may cause deterioration. Food cannot be digested properly. Organs and tissues are damaged. Sleep is disturbed. Anxiety, depression, and fatigue occur more often and for longer periods. Stressful events are more difficult to manage. The breathing process affects all aspects of daily life.

Proper breathing involves taking long, deep breaths that expand the diaphragm fully and push sufficient quantities of air through the lungs. During times of stress, breathing becomes shallow and oxygen intake is reduced. You inhale and exhale so quickly that your blood is not fully oxygenated in your lungs. When stress is prolonged, recurrent breathing patterns can be altered and chronic bad breathing habits can be established.

Deep Breathing

Deep breathing is the process of inhaling and exhaling in a way that your body intends. It's also called *diaphragmatic* breathing because you will breathe so deeply that the diaphragm expands and contracts fully. It's necessary to slow down your rate of breathing so that air can reach and saturate your blood before being exhaled.

During deep-breathing practice sessions, you may find you have difficulty remaining focused. If your attention drifts, stop the distraction and resume concentration. Try for five minutes of concentrated practice, and then stop.

Exercise

Before learning techniques to improve your breathing, it's important to assess your current breathing patterns.

1. Lie down on a bed or padded floor. Lie with your legs straight, slightly apart, and feet rolled outward. Put your arms at your sides with palms facing up. Close your eyes.

2. Notice your breathing patterns. Are you breathing through your nose or mouth?

3. Notice your jaw and throat. Are they tense or are the muscles relaxed?

4. Does your chest rise? Do your shoulders move as you breathe in and out?

5. Focus your attention on your abdomen. Does it expand fully with each breath you take in?

6. Notice other areas of the body. Do you detect tension in your arms, legs, torso, face?

Exercise

Deep breathing may be practiced sitting in a comfortable chair or in a reclining position. It's necessary to practice deep breathing on a regular basis for several weeks. While you may feel that you have learned the procedure and are getting immediate benefits, good breathing techniques become automatic only after they are practiced to the point of being overlearned.

1. Settle into a comfortable position. Loosen tight clothing.

2. Place your hands, palms down, on your abdomen.

3. Breathe through your nose or mouth, whichever is more comfortable for you.

4. Breathe in slowly. Count to three at one-second intervals as you inhale.

5. Notice that your abdomen is expanding and that your hands are being pushed outward. Your shoulders should remain motionless. Your chest will move minimally, if at all, and in concert with your abdomen.

6. Breathe out even more slowly—to the count of five, at one-second intervals. Exhale through your mouth. You will make a whooshing sound. Be sure to completely empty your lungs of air.

7. Repeat this process for five more minutes.

You may find that you feel no immediate effect from the relaxation exercise. It's tempting to give up the session when this occurs. It may take a sustained effort, over time, before you notice the benefits. You would not expect that you could play a new piece of music perfectly on the first try or learn a complex new move on the basketball court without extensive effort. Deep breathing, like any other new skill, requires practice.

Plan to practice once or twice each day. Make time in your schedule to practice. Treat your training time as importantly as any other personal task in your day. If you seriously devote yourself to this practice, you will be able to change your breathing habit in three to six weeks.

Tapping Exercise

As an adult with ADD, you may find it difficult to remain stationary for the length of the breathing practice session—even five minutes! Martha Davis, Elizabeth Eshelman, and Matthew McKay describe a technique very suited to ADDers in their excellent resource guide, *The Relaxation & Stress Reduction Workbook.* Try the next exercise.

Exercise

Use the following steps to practice deep breathing if you find it hard to sit still for five minutes.

1. Standing, sitting, or reclining, place your hands at your sides.

2. Inhale slowly to a count of three, spaced one second apart.

3. As you inhale, use your fingertips to gently tap your chest. Move your hands around your chest as you tap.

4. Tap your chest with your palms.

5. Exhale slowly to a count of five, spaced one second apart.

6. Repeat the exercise for five minutes.

7. After repeating the exercise in tapping your chest a few times, tap other areas, such as your back, throat, or face. Focus your tapping on areas where you carry tension.

The importance of practice can't be overemphasized. Once learned, you will be able to quickly instruct yourself to slow and deepen your breathing. During times of stress, you will have an immediate, effective technique for increasing your emotional control. In addition to daily practice sessions, it's important to check your breathing throughout the day. When you catch yourself in the quick, shallow breathing, correct it by taking a few slow and deep breaths.

Link your self-checks on your breathing techniques to regularly occurring daily situations. For example, checking your breathing as you cross the doorway to work will help you to relax and remember to remain calm. It's useful, too, to check your breathing patterns before entering any stressful situation.

Picture Yourself on a Desert Island . . .

Visualization is a process as natural as breathing. Like breathing, visualization can be used to help you regulate your moods. It is a particularly good technique for adults with ADD. When using your imagination, you are not relying on verbal skills or auditory processing. Instead, you are using visual skills and creative processes that are often real talents for people with ADD.

Some people report difficulty conjuring up an image and then following it with related images. But, in truth, everybody visualizes. Each time you recall a memory, you are visualizing. Your visual memory may consist of a snapshot, or you may remember long sequences of scenes. If you can create a visual memory, whether brief or extended, you can visualize. You can learn to develop this skill and use it to enhance your life. Visualization is a widely applicable skill. It can be used to calm and control emotions in the present. It can be used in the present to improve performance in the future. Visualization has also been used effectively to let people visit their past and to adjust emotional reactions to it.

Visualization for Relaxation

You can use visualization to reduce stress. Your imagination can help you to overcome feelings of frustration and replace them with a calm feeling. When you have quieted your emotional reaction to a stressful event, you can then take a cleaner, thoughtful approach to solving the problem you face.

Cas is a world traveler. The restlessness caused by his ADD has led him to some exciting places. He has seen amazing sites, and then, in his imagination, he can travel back to favorite places when he needs a relaxing escape. Cas is particularly fond of a winter vacation to the Caribbean island of St. John. One particular day is so vivid for him that he easily bumps it back from memory when he needs to relax. Here is Cas's visualization:

"I'm sitting on the warm sand on the right side of the bay. The sand is fine and almost white in the sunlight. The water of the bay stretches out as far as I can see. Palm trees surround the bay and are motionless. I can feel the hot afternoon sun. Muscle tension is melting away. Occasionally a breeze passes, and it's warm and reminds me that I'm far from home. I dig my fingers and toes into the sand, and the softness is soothing. The water is a deep blue, reflecting the cloudless sky. I close my eyes and remember the cool feeling and buoyancy of the salt water. I remember, too, snorkeling earlier in the morning and seeing

Exercise

Attention to a few points will greatly enhance your use of the visualization technique. Each time you practice visualization, assess yourself for each of the following items as if you were using a pilot's checklist before take-off.

1. Settle into a comfortable place. You may choose to recline or sit in a slightly padded chair.

2. Loosen tight clothing.

3. Close your eyes. It's important to screen out all distractions and to use your eyes for creating visual images.

4. Use all of your senses in the image you create. Imagine the sight, smell, feel (even taste) of your scenes.

5. Scan your body for any muscle tension and let it go.

6. Take a few, slow deep breaths.

7. Clean your mind of any thoughts.

8. If thoughts intrude, don't worry. Try to let them go and return your attention to deep breathing and muscle relaxation.

the banks of pink coral and schools of blue and yellow fish. I feel slightly drowsy and completely relaxed."

Curtis was a happy, very active child. Ever since he can remember he ran everywhere—to school, to the neighborhood playground—everywhere. As an adult he's continued his passion for running, and it is an essential part of his ADD coping plan. But he can't run every day, and he needs other stress-reducing techniques to add to his program. Curtis tried visualizing quiet scenes on the beach and lying in the sand, but all he thought of was running on the beach, and he couldn't relax. Curtis needed to be moving. Curtis developed imagery using running, and it worked. He could then call upon the following description when he needed a break:

"I am tying the laces of my most worn-in, favorite running shoes. I am taking the first slow jogging steps to the end of the driveway and then turn left. I feel a lungful of fresh, moist air. It feels great. This will be a good run. I am jogging down the street and noticing the familiar houses and cars on the street. I'm turning right into the park and feel warmed up now. A runner passes me going in the opposite direction, and we nod to each other. I'm feeling loose and am beginning to speed up. It feels good. The park is beautiful today. I notice how green the grass is, the trees in full bloom, and the sky an azure blue. I swerve to miss some kids fooling around on their bicycles. Other runners pass and nod. I know I'm running well. Nothing hurts. I'm picking up more speed. The lawns are mown, and the smell of the freshly cut grass is all around. I feel alive. My breathing is heavy and I can feel the air as it enters my mouth. I'm heading down the hill and through the wrought-iron park gates. The sounds of the street are noticeable. I am slowing down and watching the path more carefully. I'm rounding the corner to my street and slowing down. I'm now walking the last few yards to my driveway. I've had a good run. I feel good."

Both Cas and Curtis found personal experiences that they could return to again and again. Because their visualizations were based on real memories, they had a vividness that increased their effectiveness. Curtis and Cas chose solitary experiences. You can choose to be alone or with others in your visualization. The key is to create a scene that you can lose yourself in and one that creates emotionally quieting feelings for you.

Practice relaxation using visualization on a daily basis. Your sessions will typically last ten to twenty minutes. You will experience tension reduction almost immediately and increase your sense of calm as the session progresses. Over time, though, you will improve your skill. You will find that you relax more quickly and reach deeper states of relaxation.

Brief Vacations

You can use the visualization techniques as a stress reducer at a moment's notice. If you are experiencing stress at any time, take a brief vacation by closing your eyes and visualizing a relaxing scene for ten to twenty seconds.

- Picture yourself whizzing down a ski slope, walking on the beach at sunset, or gardening in your own backyard.

- Keep a picture of a vacation scene on your desk or bureau to help trigger the memory. Through brief visualization you will have successfully distracted yourself from the stress of the moment, relaxed your mind and body, and given yourself more energy to cope with the present event.

Physical Exercise: The Natural Medication

Ed Hallowell and John Ratey, authors of *Driven to Distraction,* strongly advocate the use of exercise for mood management. John Ratey notes how often ADDers enjoy jogging and running—even marathons. Regular exercise is a natural medication for the mood variability common in ADD. The authors wonder whether ADDers would need medication if they could exercise three or four times a day. Exercise channels the physical restlessness of ADD into positive outlets and increases the body's metabolism for much longer than the time spent exercising. The result is reduced body tension, anxiety, and surprisingly, less fatigue. Exercise also benefits psychological health. Thomas Plante notes in *Healthline* magazine that regular exercise can relieve mild to moderate depression and improve self-esteem and self-confidence.

Exercise

Think of your past experiences and choose one that brings back pleasant memories.

1. Identify the scene: _____

2. Identify the sensory experiences of the memory:

   Touch _____

   Taste _____

   Smell _____

   Sight _____

   Sound _____

3. Practice now for ten to twenty minutes the step of relaxation and visualization.

4. Daily practice:

   a. What time each day will I practice relaxation? _____

   b. Where will I practice? _____

   c. How long will I practice? _____

   d. What will I do to eliminate external distractions? _____

   e. What will I do to eliminate internal distractions? _____

Aerobic vs. Nonaerobic Exercise

There are two forms of exercise, aerobic and nonaerobic. Aerobic means *air* and the two forms of exercise differ in the way air is consumed. Aerobic exercise requires a sustained effort over time. Nonaerobic exercise is made up of stop-and-start effort.

Aerobic exercises include running, jogging, bicycling, rowing, walking, swimming, cross-country skiing, jumping rope, stair climbing, tennis, soccer, and basketball. Nonaerobic exercises include golf, weight lifting, housework, and yard work.

When the lungs are worked vigorously for a sustained period of time, as in aerobic exercise, body chemistry is changed. Chemical activity in the brain increases and endorphins are increased. Endorphins are natural painkillers that give you a feeling of calm. At the same time, mental alertness as well as your metabolism increase.

To achieve aerobic exercise, the biggest muscles in the body, the leg and buttock muscles, must be worked. Other muscle groups just don't have the capacity to cause the lungs to work hard enough to set off this chain reaction. The muscles also must work at a certain intensity level for a sustained period of time. Intensity level is determined by a percentage of maximum heart rate, which is determined by age.

Exercise

If you're not a regular exerciser, use some or all of the following techniques to incorporate exercise into your mood-management plan.

1. Find a partner. When you exercise with someone else, you get the additional benefits of a social relationship. You also have someone to encourage you on those off days. Exercise with someone at your level of fitness. It's not usually a good idea for men and women to work out together since men have more muscle and less body fat. It's typically harder for the woman to keep up (and the man may have to slow down, which lessens the benefit for him). Don't let anyone push you to work harder than you can.

   Who can I exercise with? _____

2. Always start slowly; even less than twelve minutes is OK to start. If you're in any doubt about your ability to exercise, see your doctor first. You can build up to more time.

   How long (give a range) do I want to exercise? _____

3. Develop a variety of exercises. You may get tired of the same exercise day after day. Also, you need exercises that won't be derailed by the weather.

   What exercise will I do? _____

4. Keep a record of your exercise. A daily graph or log provides useful, positive feedback. Make the graph or log cumulative. Add the minutes of each day to the previous day's total. In this way, you can see your progress as the line goes up. Computer programs are available for monitoring the time, type, and amount of exercise you do. Build your exercise monitoring into your daily routine.

5. Set aside time each day (or at least three days per week) for exercise. Write it into your daily schedule. Once you get hooked, you'll not forget again.

   What days are best for me to exercise? _____

   What time? _____

If you have been doing aerobic exercise regularly, you know the benefits. When exercising, you can feel the cobwebs clearing out of your brain and muscles. You're probably addicted to this healthy pastime and need no further convincing. If you've yet to experience the magnificent feelings of a good workout, you may need some of the following pointers to get started.

Two to Soothe Your Soul

Any discussion of mood management would be incomplete without including two of the greatest human gifts: music and laughter.

Music

Music is as old as the human race. Humans have demonstrated that they will create music wherever they are and with whatever is available to them. Music, based on rhythm, provides repetitive sounds which are soothing to the human spirit. Music is used in all human endeavors that require an emotional response. Through music, feelings can be manipulated—passions can be stirred, sadness and laughter can be induced. You can use music, too, to control or create your own moods.

Laughter

Laughter is a natural form of relaxation. When you laugh, muscles are tightened, held tight for a moment, and then relaxed. This process of tensing and relaxing creates a calmer

Exercise

Use the following questions to think about what kind of music you like and how and where you can use it to manage your moods.

1. Choose the type of music that suits you. You do not need quiet, classical music to relax. Some ADDers use loud rock music to unwind, and it works for them.

   What music chills me out? _____

2. Sing. Whistling, humming, or singing a tune can refocus your thoughts and change a mood. Get in the shower, your car, or any private place and sing as loudly as you can.

   Can I sing in the shower? _____

   Can I sing in the car during my commute? _____

3. Keep music on in the background while you are working. Music can help drown out auditory distractions. By helping to keep you on an even emotional keel, music can aid concentration.

   Can I listen to music at work? _____

   Home? _____

4. Play music while you are practicing deep breathing and visualization. It can help you to relax and again, reduce distractions.

   Will music help my relaxation work? _____

   What music will I use? _____

physical state. Also, air is exhaled during laughter and breathing becomes deep—more diaphragmatic. Finally, it's not possible to focus on worrisome thoughts when finding the humor in some event.

Exercise

Find opportunities to put laughter in your life with the following suggestions.

1. Look for the lighter side of your experiences. Try to find the humor in the situation. If you can't, ask someone else to point out the absurdity of the moment.

   Who could I contact for some light feedback on my situation? _____

2. Have a list of funny movies, books, or cartoons that you can turn to when you're feeling stressed. What's the funniest movie?

   book? _____

   cartoon I've seen? _____

3. Get together with friends, keeping drugs and alcohol out of the situation. Learn to relax and enjoy yourself without them.

   Who would be good contacts for relaxed socializing? _____

4. Go to a comedy club.

   What comedy clubs are local? _____

5. Watch some children or animals play.

   Where can I got to see children play? _____

   Would I rent a nature movie? _____

All in a Night's Sleep

Getting a good night's sleep is essential for maintaining a stable mood. But many people with ADD have problems with sleep. ADDers often report that they can't settle down to sleep at night. They are frequently kept up by racing thoughts. The quiet of night often releases pent-up emotions, and the ADDer may lie awake ruminating over the day's events. ADDers also may have difficulty staying asleep. Most people wake up occasionally during the night, but for adults with ADD this may be a nightly problem. Waking up several times during

1. Do I often have difficulty getting to sleep? Yes _____ No _____

2. Do I often have difficulty staying asleep? Yes _____ No _____

3. What time do I usually go to bed? _____

4. What activities do I do just before going to bed? _____

a sleep cycle interferes with the brain's chemistry, which undergoes regular changes during sleep. Without sound sleep, it's difficult to maintain alertness during the following day, and many ADDers report daytime sleepiness. Feeling tired also increases irritability and emotional instability.

Developing a bedtime routine can greatly improve your sleep habits. Going to bed at a regular time will help condition your body to become tired at night. It's also helpful to get up at a set time—every day, including weekends. Daytime napping can greatly interfere with nighttime sleep. But if you must nap, don't do it in the evening hours. Caffeine, alcohol, and some ADD medications can disturb sleep. Be sure to monitor when you use these substances so that they don't interfere with your need to slow yourself down enough to sleep. Getting yourself to stop thinking may be the most difficult sleep habit to build. It can help to have a favorite movie to view in your mind, or use visualization as a relaxing activity. If you get distracted, keep returning your mind to your chosen thoughts. Eventually, you'll concentrate.

Exercise

Take some time to answer the following questions about sleeping habits to develop a bedtime routine.

1. What time will I go to bed each night? _____

2. What relaxing activity can I do before going to bed? _____

3. What time will I have my last cup of coffee? _____

   alcoholic drink? ADD medication? _____

4. What thought-stopping story/visualization can I use? _____

Summary

- Adults with ADD often experience mood swings. Shifts from feeling high to very low can occur within a day. Sometimes there is no apparent reason for the shift. Other times a minor disappointment can trigger a strong response.

- Developing awareness of mood states is the first step toward managing them; then you can work on some techniques that help bring them under control:

  Learning to breathe slowly and deeply from the diaphragm is a useful technique for calming anxiety.

  Visualizing a pleasant experience can be used to relieve stress and improve mood.

  Exercising is one of the best ways to elevate moods and constructively channel the restlessness of ADD.

  Listening to music helps many ADDers to alleviate stress.

  Looking for opportunities to laugh takes your mind of worries and increases relaxation.

  Developing a bedtime routine improves your sleep, which means you'll be more alert and emotionally stable.

9

Impulsivity:

How to Recognize Why and When You Lose Control

Impulsivity is a relatively new addition to our understanding of ADD. It was included in the definition of ADD developed in 1980. The importance of impulsivity to our understanding and treatment of ADD can't be diminished by its late inclusion. Impulsivity may be the most difficult of all the ADD symptoms. Unmanaged, impulsivity can cause trouble.

Difficulty controlling impulses is a pervasive problem for adult ADDers. Problems may be small, such as the urge to rush through a job and "just get it done," or the inability to resist buying that jacket you don't really need. Other problems with impulse control can be serious, such as the inability to resist high-stakes gambling, verbally exploding at the boss, or buying a car on a whim. Impulsivity, too, is related to physical aggression, crime, and violence. And aggression in children with ADD is one of the predictors of poor adjustment in adult life.

Impulsivity is born of a low tolerance for frustration. The overstimulation felt during frustration can be hard to bear, and ADDers often seek relief by just doing something—anything—to lower the frustration. ADDers may blurt out something to reduce their tension or engage in some activity that will distract them from the frustration of the moment. ADDers find it hard to wait, be patient, or "just go with the flow." They want action *now*.

Impulsivity is the tendency to act too quickly and without thinking. Impulsivity involves not being able to stop an action before it starts or to stop or change a behavior once it's started. These urges to act seem independent of reason. ADDers often know the consequences of their behavior but still have great difficulty controlling it. Russell Barkley has said that ADD isn't about not knowing what to do, but it is about doing what you know.

The cycle of frustration, acting impulsively, and then feeling more frustration about not controlling your own behavior may be replayed over and over. If your impulsivity involves risky behavior—such as spending large amounts of money, engaging in unprotected sex, drinking and/or taking drugs and driving—it's important to seek professional help immediately. The high-risk behavior will require separate treatment from ADD. If your impulsivity is not causing risk to yourself or others, you can develop skills to help you put on the brakes when needed. Medications are often very helpful in impulse control problems, and you should discuss this possibility with your doctor. When impulsivity is managed, like problems with hyperactivity and attention, it can result in additional assets for you in your life. Impulsivity can become ambition and a drive to help you reach your goals.

Becoming Aware of Your Impulsive Behavior

As with many of the other behaviors discussed in this book, it's first necessary to be aware that it occurs before you can learn to manage your impulsivity. But, almost by definition, impulsivity occurs before you can think.

> Julie, a 24-year-old nursing student, has a number of impulse control issues. She was a hyperactive tomboy as a child, always making up new games to play. As an adult she talks incessantly. She has a quick wit, and her peers love the caustic remarks she can make about her teachers and supervisors. She can also be brutally blunt with peers. She'll tell a friend exactly what she thinks about her friends, clothes, and so on. She always laughs when she makes these remarks and gets away with it by catching others off guard. Julie has seen many a friend over the years burst into tears and run from the room. People are careful around her—a little afraid. Julie has the habit of throwing things. She's lonely a lot of the time. She's hyper and chain-smokes. She can rarely just put things down. She tosses things across the room, hoping they will hit the target. She is a binge-eater when home alone. Ice cream is like alcohol for her. It soothes her jangled nerves and temporarily distracts her from her constant feeling that things are exploding all around her. Julie hates the way she lives, but she just can't get a grip on her caustic tongue and the feelings that her outbursts create for her.

Julie lives in a constant state of high stimulation. She is hyper by nature but she's also balancing school, nurse training, and work. She feels as if she's on fast-forward and completely unable to calm or control herself.

Once you are aware of what behaviors you are likely to act on impulsively, it's important to assess the circumstances when impulsivity will occur.

Typically, ADDers act impulsively when overstimulated. When you are rushing to get something done or when a lot is happening around you, it's easy to get caught up in the commotion and let down your guard. It's also harder to control impulses when you are tired or if you have been drinking alcohol. Females, too, may have increased difficulty with impulse control during hormonal fluctuations.

Exercise

To get a start on managing your own impulses, first take a brief inventory of areas where you are likely to lose control. Place a check mark next to each behavior where you feel you have had difficulty controlling impulses.

_____ driving   _____ using drugs   _____ engaging in sex

_____ gambling   _____ spending money   _____ losing your temper

_____ blurting things out _____ eating   _____ physically hurting
                                                                    yourself

Now, take a minute and review the list. Don't be surprised or worried if there are a lot of check marks. Progress can be made in most areas over time. Next pick one behavior area for further work now, and write it down here: _____

Avoiding Temptation

Once you are aware of which behaviors are likely to slip out of your control and the conditions creating this lapse, you can begin to avoid these pitfalls. For each behavior you identified as problematic, make a list of the conditions in which you lost control. Commit your lists to memory. Look at the lists on a daily basis. The more familiar you become with the conditions for impulsivity, the greater your chances for recognizing them before you lose control.

Exercise

Think of the last five times you had difficulty with your chosen impulse control issue. Were any of the following occurring?

_____ a lot of noise   _____ many people around _____ being alone

_____ certain person(s) present _____ rushing   _____ feeling tired

_____ hormonal fluctuations   _____ drinking alcohol   _____ feeling ill

_____ in transition from one _____ feeling depressed/sad
        place to another

For each of the impulse behaviors you checked in the previous exercise, assess the conditions in which you lost control.

Next, eliminate as many standing temptations as you can. Do not keep alcohol in the house if impulse drinking is a problem. Many people want to prove that they can control themselves in the face of temptation. This stage comes much later—if ever. For now, avoid costly situations. If you have trouble resisting the urge to stop at the liquor store on the way home from work, take a new route, even if it's a bit longer. One of the hardest temptations to avoid will be certain people with whom you associate your loss of impulse control. You will need to avoid them, or at least being with them in high-risk situations. It's best to tell them why you're not as available as you were. Be prepared, though, for a barrage of excuses, jokes, even threats, as they try to put blame back on you.

Exercise

What changes can I make to reduce temptation?

For example: Do I need to see some friends for lunch instead of dinner or after work?

Should I go to the gym for thirty minutes before going straight home after a stressful day?

Should I make a habit of going to the gym instead of going out to party when I'm tired?

_____

_____

_____

Getting Feedback

When impulsivity involves making a decision, the best plan is to deliberately impose a delay. Again, awareness that you are about to lose it is necessary. If, for example, you have an overwhelming urge to buy a Harley: *stop,* think, and talk it over with someone else. ADDers are often quite independent in their actions and resist advice to "talk things over" with someone else. But *everyone,* from the president consulting his cabinet on down, needs advice. Getting advice is getting more information. *You* will still be the person to make the final decision. Getting feedback from more than one person is advisable. You can catch someone on an off day and not get really good information. Also, by consulting more than one person, you slow the process down even further and give yourself additional time to think.

It's also a good idea to give yourself at least twenty-four hours before acting on your impulse. Again, if you're thinking of putting $10,000 down on a new motorcycle, take a break—a long one. Twenty-four hours is allotted because it will typically involve a period of sleep. You will be relieved at how much your urge has decreased if you sleep on it for a night.

Exercise

Keep a record like the following for your impulsive behaviors.

1. When I'm fighting temptation to _____ I'll first talk it over with

_____ and _____ .

2. Mentally record the time you have the urge to engage in the impulsive behavior, and note when your twenty-four hour period is up.

Also, think of alternatives for the money you're spending impulsively—what about a trip to Europe, or even New Zealand?

Slowing Down

The ADDer's mind and body move at a fast pace. When you're going at a high rate of speed, it's difficult to make thoughtful decisions. It's as if you're on automatic, and actions occur without your thinking or even realizing they're happening. Speeding, then, is a prime setup for impulsive behavior. When you're going too fast and things seem out of your control, it's important to slow down *before* you act impulsively.

Be aware of when you're rushing. Keep some calming activity handy so that you can quickly take a break and slow yourself down. You may need to keep a set of worry beads at your desk. You can take a minute and stretch your muscles or do deep breathing. Or you can tell yourself to slow down your rate of talking and moving. Take a walk and deliberately slow your pace. Be conscious of your voice, and slow yourself down to half your usual speed. Finally, ask a friend or colleague to let you know when you're speeding.

Exercise

Take a moment to write down the activities and people you can count on to help slow you down.

1. What activity can I keep handy to distract and calm me

at work? _____

at home? _____

other _____

2. Who can I ask to let me know when I'm going too fast

at work? _____

at home? _____

other _____

Controlling Urges

When an urge strikes, you need to be prepared. First identify your urge—call it by name: "There's that old chocolate craving again" or "I can feel my urge to drink building up." Labeling an urge helps to put some distance between you and the craving. Next, have a substitute behavior ready to act on. Find some behavior that is incompatible with the craving but one that you can reasonably expect to do. For example, if you're craving a spending spree at the mall, you may not be able to successfully distract yourself by cleaning the bathroom. Think of something that can calm you down without causing you further problems. If you're having a chocolate craving fit, try playing a computer game or doing something that will absorb your attention until the urge passes.

It is important that the distraction you choose be readily available. If you have to hunt for the mystery novel you've been reading, you may give up and give in to your urge to surf the home-shopping channels.

In addition to naming your urge, use other forms of self-talk to help you through those excruciating moments as the urge builds. Keep saying to yourself, "It will pass." And it will. If you do not succumb to your cravings, they get weaker over time. Occasionally, they'll come back in some full-blown form, but if you resist, they will pass.

Using Visualization to Control Impulses

In addition to lowering your stress level, visualization can be used to train impulse control. Many top athletes use visualization to train themselves to concentrate and control body movements. Top golfers, ice skaters, and basketball players have written about their successful use of visualization. Visualization is a way to practice a skill. Using your imagination, you can picture yourself controlling what you say and do. You can see yourself handling problems with ease. The benefit of this practice is that when actually confronted with the situation, you can perform as you want to. You can practice resisting peer pressure to drink, the urge to get angry at the boss, the urge to throw your clothes in a big pile in the middle of the bedroom floor—you can even practice getting to sleep at night.

Chapter 8 describes visualization techniques and gives some examples. You should select a quiet time and place where you won't be interrupted to practice visualization. Relax your body, clear your mind, and begin to see yourself moving through real-life scenes and

Exercise

To reinforce your awareness, complete these steps:

1. The names of my most troublesome urges are _____ ,
_____ , _____ , _____ .

2. For each urge, identify an incompatible behavior that you can do until the craving passes:

Urge   Alternative Behavior

a. _____   _____

b. _____   _____

c. _____   _____

d. _____   _____

3. What can I repeat to myself over and over until the urge passes?

a. _____

b. _____

c. _____

Exercise

Practice visualizing resisting your own urge to act impulsively. Imagine yourself in the situation in which you are likely to need to control an impulsive urge. Put as many details into your thoughts as you can.

Now practice visualizing resisting others who are urging you to do something impulsive. Imagine that you turn them down without getting angry. Practice using humor or just disinterest as they urge you to do something impulsive.

controlling yourself as you want to. You may get distracted, but don't worry, just return your thoughts to visualization and continue. Like any skill, the more you practice, the easier it gets. Practice visualization daily for a few weeks. You'll be able to visualize faster and more completely with practice.

Stopping Once You Start

There are times when you catch yourself in an impulsive act after you have started. You look down and find yourself halfway through a bowl of ice cream or bottle of beer. ADDers find it difficult to stop at this point. The problem occurs in what you say to yourself. Typically, you will chastise yourself for starting but then feel that the damage is done, so why stop now? But it is important to stop once you start. By continuing, you are giving yourself permission to be impulsive. You can weaken the impulsive urge by breaking it at any stage. Have an alternative activity to switch into. By changing to a nonimpulsive behavior, the substitute activity will come to be associated with the urge, and over time, you increase your chances of choosing the alternative behavior instead of the impulsive one. Your alternative must be easily available. Some people choose walking, taking a pen apart, or doodling. Also, if you stop halfway through, you're still improving over last time!

What alternative act can I have ready when I need to stop an impulsive behavior?

_____

Understanding Anger

ADDers get angry frequently and quickly. Anger is a common experience due to the flood of emotion accompanying ADD. The feeling of being overwhelmed and frustrated often leads to anger. Depending on your personality, you may bury these feelings—which leads to depression—or you may let your anger go in impulsive outbursts.

It's true that everyone gets angry. Frustration and disappointment occur in every life. Problems occur when anger becomes pervasive. An ADDer who is angry all of the time is adding physical and mental stress to an already demanding life. And if you're feeling generally angry, you will find situations to be angry about. Angry feelings can be set off so quickly that the ADDer does not have time to assess the emotion. Impulsivity, combined with the powerful feeling of anger, can lead to devastating results in a personal or work situation.

ADDers are impatient. Again, there are so many things going on in the ADDer's mind that it's difficult to find the time to sort them all out. The person with ADD just wants to get on with things and feels that there isn't time to explain to others. This impatience often leads to snapping at questions or barking orders to others. The ADDer often is not angry with the person receiving these attacks. It's just that the frustration level has boiled over at that point, and any person present is likely to get an earful.

People will be as angry as others let them. Angry outbursts require reinforcement to be maintained. If others back down when faced with an ADDer's anger, the anger has been rewarded. Rewarded anger grows—if verbal attacks are accepted today, then throwing things, making threats, and acting aggressively may develop over time. It's critical to derail anger in its early stages when it's much easier to manage.

Many angry people blame others. They feel that someone got them mad; that if some act had not occurred, they would not have been so angry. Nothing could be further from the truth. You are responsible for getting angry and for what you do with it. You have choices, first to decide *if* you want to be angry and *then* how you will handle it.

What Triggers Your Anger?

Like other impulsive acts, it's important to be aware of what triggers your anger. When you are knowledgeable about who, what, when, where, and why you become angry, you are in a better position to catch yourself before you get really angry and before you are likely to act impulsively on it.

Exercise

Make copies of the daily anger log shown on the next page. For now, fill in the time and place, what happened, and the intensity (high, low, medium, or a scale from 1 to 10) of times you were angry during one week. Then look it over to see where your triggers occur. Do they occur in the morning when you're not quite awake, at work when you're rushed, or at home where family members make demands on your attention? In the next two sections, you will learn how to recognize the underlying emotions in anger and how your interpretation of events influences your angry feelings.

What Are You Really Feeling?

Anger always disguises another emotion. It covers up what you are truly feeling. Anger is a defense against more vulnerable feelings such as hurt, loss, and powerlessness. To really understand and manage anger, you must recognize what's underneath it. This takes courage because it's not easy to see yourself as vulnerable. But if you can recognize and accept less powerful feelings, you can resolve anger and deal more effectively with what's really bothering you.

Jessie has a pervasive problem with anger. As a child he had trouble playing with other boys. If he lost a game, he would stomp off in an angry fit. He had

Daily Anger Log

Date _____   Time _____   Place _____

What Happened _____

_____

Intensity of Anger _____

Interpretation of What Happened _____

Underlying Emotion _____

Date _____   Time _____   Place _____

What Happened _____

_____

Intensity of Anger _____

Interpretation of What Happened _____

Underlying Emotion _____

Date _____   Time _____   Place _____

What Happened _____

_____

Intensity of Anger _____

Interpretation of What Happened _____

Underlying Emotion _____

tantrums at home, too, when asked to clean his room, sit up at the dinner table, or take out the trash. His outbursts began as yelling and progressed to slamming doors and then throwing items in his room. By high school he had gotten into some fistfights. He settled down in adulthood but is still known as someone with a temper. He learned not to drink because he became very impulsive and aggressive at those times. Jessie tries hard to control his anger, but it seems to come out of nowhere. He can just wake up feeling irritable and angry. Without knowing it, Jessie feels his anger by the way he perceives others. When someone cuts him off at a stoplight, he tells himself that the other driver is a jerk. His anger is then justified. He's resentful of his supervisor at work, who gives him a lot of tedious, unimportant work. He feels the boss is playing a power game, deliberately trying to do him in. What Jessie doesn't realize is that all of these events make him feel small, powerless. Since it's so difficult to acknowledge this vulnerable feeling, he compensates with the powerful feeling of anger. If Jessie realized what he is feeling, he would come up with some constructive ways to assert himself at work—to get his work recognized and to gain power and control of his life.

Exercise

This exercise will help you begin to identify the feelings beneath your anger.

1. Think of the most recent experience with anger you have had. Describe it here:

_____

_____

_____

2. What did you feel underneath the anger? _____ hurt, _____ fear, _____ loneliness, _____ powerlessness, _____ loss, _____ rejection, _____ worthlessness, _____ injustice

3. Using your daily anger log, identify the real feeling underneath the anger for each situation identified for the day.

Jessie interprets the behavior of others as dangerous to him. He thinks his supervisor is trying to undermine him and even the driver at the stoplight has no regard for him as a person with rights, too. Jessie gives himself every excuse to be angry. He doesn't consider that others

Exercise

Use this exercise to identify your interpretations of others' behavior that are contributing to your anger.

1. Think of three times today (or in recent days) that you have been angry. Identify your interpretation of the other person's behavior.

   What Happened   Why They Did It

   a. _____   _____

   b. _____   _____

   c. _____   _____

2. Using your daily anger log, identify your interpretation of the behavior of others. Consider other, less threatening, reasons for behavior.

may be distracted and thoughtless, but not trying to hurt him—or any of a number of reasons for the inconsiderate behavior of others.

How to Stop the Escalation

When anger starts to build, it's important to stop it. The longer you let it go, the more difficult it will be to manage and the more you risk taking some impulsive action. Also, you are rehearsing poor anger management. You are getting familiar, and comfortable, with escalation.

Take a break. If you feel your anger escalating and can't talk yourself down on the spot, take a break. Remove yourself from the people and situation around you. Tell others exactly what you're doing. Tell them you want to take a few minutes and calm down. Once out of the heated situation, you'll need to engage in some calming activity. If you don't, you'll continue to think about your anger, your reasons for being angry, and you won't be able to cool down. Once out of harm's way, do something that will distract you and reduce your level of arousal. You may engage in deep breathing, exercise, creative visualization; or simply read, play a game, or do one of the activities you have written down to distract and calm you.

Using Signals

Escalation can happen quickly. You may find yourself in a full-blown rage before you can even begin to think. This process of escalation will slow down with practice. But until you conquer it, you may need someone or something outside yourself to tell you to slow down. Ask a friend or colleague to give you a signal when you're beginning to escalate. At home, too, you can have a family member let you know that it's time for a break. As difficult as it may seem to take advice from others when an anger attack is building, it gets easier with practice. You can set up your own signals. If you catch a glimpse of your reflection in a window or mirror, note how you appear. If your brow is furrowed, lips tight, you're getting angry, and that can be your signal to take a break. Some ADDers put red dots on their wristwatch, desk clock, kitchen clock, too. When you see red, stop and think if you need to take a break. Take one. If you're not escalating out of control, that's OK. No harm in practicing.

Exercise

Imagine a recent incident when you became very angry, and then answer the following questions.

1. Where could I have gone to take a break? _____

2. How could I have explained my leaving to others? _____

3. What activity could I have engaged in to clam down? _____

Exercise

Set up some signals you can use to stop the escalation of anger:

1. Who can I ask to signal me when I'm beginning to escalate

   at work? _____

   at home? _____

   other _____

2. What signal can we use

   at work? _____

   at home? _____

   other _____

3. What signal can I set up for myself to take a break when needed? _____

How to Resolve Anger

Once you have broken the escalation of anger, it's important to return to the situation with a new strategy. You want to come out of the situation with a good solution for yourself but one that doesn't damage others. To figure out this constructive ending, begin to ask questions. It's important that you do so with a neutral tone of voice. If you develop an angry edge, take another break. Ask questions about why the other people involved feel so strongly. Listen to their answers and try to understand another position. Ask if they can see any other solution to the problem. If you develop an angry edge, take a break. Keep the dialogue going until some mutual feelings and even solutions begin to emerge. If no final solution can be reached, thank others for talking and suggest another time to talk further.

Exercise

Think back to a recent disagreement with others. Replay the event in your imagination. Picture yourself calmly asking questions and imagining the answers. Keep up the dialogue until a solution is reached.

For example, your wife wants to spend some extra cash on repainting the back wall of the house. You feel that you need a vacation and should spend the money on a weekend away.

You: You seem to feel strongly about painting the back wall.

Wife: You never think of anything practical. All you want to do is play.

You: I like to have fun. But right now I want to know how important this is to you.

Wife: It's very important. The place looks like it's falling down.

You: I can see your point. It does look shabby. But I think it would do us good to get away. Is there anyway we can do both?

Wife: Maybe we could stay at my sister's cottage some weekend when she's not there.

You: That sounds good. I'll get someone to work on the house, if you'll call your sister.

If anger has gotten out of control and damage has been done, it's important to make amends. Don't let a wrong go unresolved. If you have hurt someone's feelings, apologize. You don't need to grovel, but simply state that you're sorry that someone was hurt. If property was damaged, offer to pay for it. Your apologies and offers of restitution may not be accepted. That's OK. You have taken the final step in breaking the destructive cycle of anger. It's also never too late to right a wrong. Even if the damage was done years ago, you can still offer to

Exercise

Think back to a situation when you acted destructively out of anger. How can you offer to repair the damages?

Situation: _____

_____

Restitution: _____

_____

make the situation better. By paying your debts, emotional or monetary, you take responsibility for *your* anger and actions.

Summary

- Impulsivity may be the most difficult ADD trait to manage. It is related to a low tolerance for frustration, and often occurs when you are overstimulated or when you are tired, sick, or sad.

- Becoming aware of impulsive action is an essential first step in overcoming it. Once you identify where and why you are likely to lose control, you can use a variety of techniques to change:

    Avoid people, places, and substances that are associated with your impulsive behavior.

    Get feedback from others about your intended action, and wait twenty-four hours before acting.

    Be aware of when you are rushing. Engage in some calming activity to slow yourself down.

    Visualize yourself resisting impulsive behavior.

    Stop an impulsive behavior even if you have begun.

- Anger combined with impulsivity can have devastating results for adults with ADD. As with other strong emotions, understanding what sets off your anger is the key to managing anger.

    Different people have different anger triggers. Become aware of what yours are.

    Anger covers up other emotions, such as fear. Be aware of what's underneath the anger.

The more anger escalates, the harder it is to manage. Take a break when you feel anger building.

Anger needs to be resolved. Deal with anger assertively by asking questions. If you have hurt someone or damage property, apologize and offer to pay for it, if necessary.

10

Learning Skills:

Identify and Build on the Skills You Already Have

The subject of learning may bring back troubled memories of school for adults with ADD. Years of hearing, "Sit still," "Pay attention," "Try harder" still ring in your ears. Many ADDers, in spite of being quite intelligent, left school early or before they reached their full learning potential. While it's possible to escape harsh words of uninformed teachers, learning can never be avoided. It's a daily experience. Learning involves taking in and using information. Each time you try a new tool or recipe, practice a sport, or read the newspaper, learning occurs. Learning involves observation, memory, and application. It takes certain skills, and with practice, you can learn how to learn. These skills are useful to you whether you are in school or planning to return, at work, or in your personal life.

Memory's Link to Learning

To use new information, you must first remember it. Many ADDers complain of having a bad memory. ADDers do remember a great deal but are often bothered by the instances when they struggle to remember. Like other ADD symptoms, memory can be inconsistent. ADDers may have a great facility for remembering some types of facts, names, and dates but great difficulty with others.

Some problems with memory are not unexpected for ADDers. Memory is controlled by the brain's frontal lobe, which has impaired functioning in ADD. Memory is made up of taking in, storing, and then retrieving information when needed. A breakdown at any stage of this chain results in memory problems. Attention is important at all three stages, which puts ADDers at a disadvantage due to problems with distractibility. Memory also requires selective attention, that is, attention to detail. Details are difficult for ADDers, again, due to distractibility. The ability to maintain attention over a period of time is important, too. For ADDers, mental fatigue can set in quickly. ADDers also are poor at self-monitoring. They may be unaware when distractions occur and their attention flags.

Techniques to improve memory have been around for centuries. Before assessing your problems with memory and developing skills to overcome them, it's useful to know a bit more about memory. First, memory is divided into three types: auditory, visual, and kinesthetic. *Auditory memory* refers to remembering what you have heard—a jingle from a commercial, criticism of your work, the screech of tires on the highway. *Visual memory* refers to what you have seen—books read, a scene from a movie, the ocean view from your last vacation. *Kinesthetic memory* is motor memory, such as remembering how to fix a lamp, how to dance, or ride a bike. An example of kinesthetic memory is the person who cannot remember a phone number until actually dialing it.

You probably know that memory also has several dimensions of time. There is immediate memory (what you're attending to right now), working memory (remembering the thought at the beginning of the chapter as you read through the text), short-term memory (remembering where you parked the car), and long-term memory (experiences from childhood). ADDers typically have good long-term memory. They can relive experiences with great detail from the past. But, immediate, working, and short-term memory may be impaired—again due to distractibility and not paying sufficient attention to the event in the first

Exercise

Check each strength you have in the following categories. Use techniques suited to your strongest memory style.

- Auditory Memory: ____ I need to follow verbal directions to do something. ____ I need to talk about something before I really understand it. ____ I learn well in lectures. ____ I need to describe a picture before I can really know it. ____ I listen to what people are saying more than their posture, expression, and so on. ____ I can remember melodies and lyrics well. ____ I get distracted by seeing things in the background.

- Visual Memory: ____ I need to follow written directions to do something. ____ I am aware of colors. ____ I need to read material to know it. ____ I don't follow lectures very well. ____ I am distracted by noise. ____ I am good at visualizing.

- Kinesthetic Memory: ____ I learn by watching others doing something. ____ I can't remember some things unless I've done them. ____ I talk with my hands a lot. ____ I'm good at sports, dancing, and so on. ____ I have a good sense of direction.

place. Finally, there is retrospective and prospective memory. *Retrospective memory* refers to recalling information from the past. It is typically verbal information, such as dates, names, events. *Prospective memory* refers to remembering what you need to do in the future, such as pick up the dry cleaning. ADDers report problems in both areas.

Memory and Stress

Stress can interfere with your ability to pay attention and to remember. One of the simplest techniques for improving memory is to reduce the amount of mental and physical tension you experience. If you are tired, anxious, or overstimulated, your mental alertness and stamina are reduced.

Exercise

Think back to a recent experience when you could not remember something—a name, what you went to the store to buy, for example. Were you feeling:

_____ tired

_____ anxious

_____ overstimulated

Review techniques in chapter 8 if any of these conditions interferes with your memory.

Remembering Names and Numbers

ADDers often report difficulty with remembering names. They struggle to remember the name of someone they just met, a movie they saw recently, or the title of a book. While these experiences do not cause serious problems, they are frustrating, and you can feel foolish when you know something but can't speak about it. As with all memory problems, there has been a breakdown in the chain from observation, to storage, to retrieval. Techniques can be applied to improve attention at all three stages.

When trying to remember the name of someone you've just met, develop some association between the name and face. The more ridiculous the association, the more it will grab your attention and aid memory. For example, Mr. Cartman has a very large nose. Try picturing a cart being pushed by a man running up and down his nose. When you see Mr. Cartman again, you'll surely notice his nose, which will trigger your memory of his name. Similarly, Mrs. Furman has a high forehead. Picture furry little men running across the expanse of forehead.

Mnemonic devices (memory aids) are useful and can be fun to make up. You may be familiar with the mnemonic for remembering the five Great Lakes: Huron, Ontario, Michigan,

Exercise

Use this exercise to practice making up memory aids.

1. Think of someone you know well. What is one outstanding facial feature? How could you associate the person's name with the face?

_____

2. Think of someone you don't know well but will see tomorrow. How could you associate that person's name with the face?

_____

Erie, and Superior. The first letter of each name combines to spell HOMES. The best devices are the ones you develop yourself. They will have the most meaning for you, and the effort you put into developing them is a memory boost itself. For example, to remember the differences between *stationery* and *stationary,* remember that only the word *paper* has an *e*; the word *stand* has only an *a* so must be spelled *stationary.*

To remember numbers, you can divide them into smaller groups. The number 26.8976 may be hard to remember, but 26-89-76 is easier. Dates can also be remembered by association. If you need to remember July 28, 1994, for example, you could associate it with one month, one day, one year after your anniversary, June 27, 1993. Any time you can link new information to existing information, you improve your chances of remembering.

To remember names and dates, always carry a small notepad with you. Write down the information as soon as you can. This is particularly important if your visual memory is strong. Then rehearse the information regularly. For example, take a few minutes at the end of each business day to review the names of the clients you have called.

Overcoming Absentmindedness

Forgetfulness is often the subject of humor. Most of us can remember stories of lovable but absentminded professors from our youth, and such characters are frequently portrayed in stories and movies. Forgetfulness usually isn't funny, though, to the person who is standing in the grocery store and can't remember what he came to buy. This type of absentmindedness can happen several times a day for the adult ADDer, and it costs time and aggravation.

As in remembering names, it's possible to remember an item or even a list of items by developing associations. For example if you need to remember to buy tissue and bread at the store, try imagining a box of tissue with bread stuffed in it instead of tissue. Longer lists can be remembered by linking the items into a story. Consider that you must pick up the dry cleaning and then go to the store for socks, milk, cookies, and coffee. Picture a stiff bag of dry cleaning sitting before a glass shaped like a sock full of milk and dipping cookies into the milk while drinking a cup of coffee. The image takes just seconds to conjure up, but it will stay with you long enough to get the job done.

If your kinesthetic memory is better than your visual memory, try imagining your route as you stop at the dry cleaners and then move on to the store. Imagine yourself walking up and down the aisles picking up socks, milk, cookies, and coffee.

Other examples of absentmindedness include misplacing necessary items and forgetting what you were going to do. Train yourself to put items in one place and only one place. It will take practice, but soon a habit will develop. If you find that you often forget to take necessary items with you, place them by the door at night, or mentally associate them with the last thing you do before you leave your home, office, or car. If the item is really important, have a duplicate. Put a spare set of house keys under a rock near the backdoor, or keep an extra pair of glasses in your desk drawer. If you have difficulty remembering why you entered a room or went to the refrigerator, form a mental image before you go. Picture the item you're going for—make it as ridiculous as you can. If you're heading to the living room to get a

Exercise

Here is some more practice in using memory aids:

1. Link the following items into a story, or picture yourself moving through the steps to accomplish the task: go to bank, buy rake at hardware store, wash car, take out trash.

_____

_____

_____

_____

2. What item(s) do you frequently forget to take with you?

_____

How can you remember them as needed? _____

3. What items do you frequently misplace? _____

_____

Where can you place these items on a routine basis? _____

_____

magazine you've started, picture the magazine flapping its pages and flying around the room. Again, if your memory is more kinesthetic, picture yourself chasing the magazine as it flaps about in all directions.

Developing a Routine to Aid Prospective Memory

Remembering to do something at a later date is prospective memory. When you forget appointments or errands you were supposed to run, it can be frustrating for you and others in your life. Forgetting a job interview, a meeting with a loan officer, or appearance in traffic court can be costly, too.

It's critical that you keep a daily schedule. You may have tried to keep track of appointments, deadlines, and so on, but gave up after a while. However, if you develop the habit of carrying your planner with you at all times, you'll become attached to it and learn to use it as a helpful tool. If you spend a lot of time at a computer, you can use a computerized version of a daily planner. Review your schedule daily and weekly. Consider this review an important activity. Write it into your schedule. Review your plans with spouse, friend, or coach until you develop the habit independently.

Developing a routine also will help you to remember some necessary activities. Always plan to stop at the bank on Fridays after work or to do the grocery shopping on Wednesdays. These activities will become habit. You'll spend a lot less time and energy dealing with emergencies if you plan a routine.

Finally, post notes to remind you of the things you need to do. Be sure to place the note where you will see it—on the steering wheel, refrigerator door, etc. There are new electronic devices that will page you—using voice or beeps—at designated times. Feel free to use these devices—they're not crutches. But you may find less need for them as you develop your schedule and routines.

Reading to Learn

ADDers often manage the demands of school in the early years, but problems emerge in high school, when the importance of reading skills increases. In the early school years, children are learning to read, but older students must read to learn. The presence of a learning disability for approximately 30 percent of ADDers can contribute to problems with reading. But ADDers often have difficulty with reading comprehension due to distractibility. ADDers begin a reading assignment with the best intentions but find that the linear process of reading just doesn't hold their attention. By the time a paragraph is finished, the main point has been lost. Rereading the material often has the same result, and after a few times, it's tempting to give up. Here are some pointers for improving your reading comprehension:

- Begin by surveying what you need to read. Take note of the headings.

- Turn each heading into a question. For example, the heading of this section is "Reading to Learn." Ask yourself questions such as, "What's the point about reading to

Exercise

If you have problems with prospective memory, this exercise will help you begin to address them.

1. Do I often forget to do things I need to do? Yes _____ No _____

2. What have I forgotten to do recently? _____

3. What scheduling system am I using to help me remember things I need to do?

   _____

   What system will I put in place for myself? _____

   When will I start? _____

4. What other things can I do to remember things I need to do?

   _____ notes _____ watch _____ alarm _____ beeper

learn?" Whenever you ask questions, you're getting actively involved with the material, and you increase your attention.

- Next read the material. If you find yourself drifting off, stop. Go back to the beginning of the paragraph.

- Take a break when needed. Even a minute or less can rest your mind and give you enough of a break to get started again. Don't be discouraged if you need frequent breaks.

- Be aware that it's more difficult to manage your attention some days than others.

- Put the material into your own words. If your memory is better for auditory information, try reciting out loud or talking to someone about what you've read. Take notes—but be sure they're in your own words.

- Skim the material again to be sure you didn't miss anything the first time through.

Note-Taking as an Aid to Learning

Whether your memory is primarily auditory or visually strong, it's important to take notes. Note-taking is not just for school. Note-taking is appropriate and important in meetings at work, visits to the doctor, support group meetings, and therapy sessions.

Exercise

Schedule time to sit down with a book you are reading for school, work, or even pleasure. Apply the techniques described in this section to improve reading comprehension.

Book title: _____

Main headings: _____

_____

_____

Questions about headings: _____

_____

_____

Summary: _____

_____

_____

_____

If you were taught to take notes by using a formal outline system in school, you can get frustrated by trying to "do it right." Feel free to develop your own system. You may want to jot down only the main points or what you've agreed to do by the end of the meeting. If you find note-taking overwhelming, you may be able to tape-record meetings. You need to ask permission of those present first. If others are taking notes in a class or meeting, ask to borrow their notes. Compare them to yours and fill in gaps in your record if there are any.

Enhance Learning by Working in Groups

Working with others on a project provides the opportunity to use many of the learning skills discussed so far. When working with others, you'll take a more active role regarding the material. Discussions of the project, different points of view, and problem-solving will occur. Each activity brings you into contact with the subject, and you'll attend and remember more.

A group can mean just one other person or more. Study groups are effective for academic work. On the job, look for, or ask for, the opportunity to work with others on a team. Even if formal groups aren't available, try to team up with one person. Select someone who complements your skills. If you're good at getting started but poor at finishing a project, work with someone who has a steadier approach.

Learning One on One: Enlist a Tutor

One of the most efficient ways to learn is to have individualized instruction. Private tutoring was the primary method of teaching for centuries. Several students working simultaneously with one teacher is a relatively modern idea. With individualized attention, your learning needs will be primary. You can move quickly through material that's easy and get more help in the tough subjects. Tutors can be a parent, spouse, or friend. You could also hire a tutor. Hourly fees range widely depending on the subject and your location. Some ADDers feel that tutors are an admission of being "dumb." They're not. They are an effective, efficient, and less painful way to learn.

Summary

- Learning involves observation, memory, and application. You may have given up on learning if you have problems remembering names, dates, and facts, because of your ADD. But you can counteract the distractibility, mental fatigue, and stress that affects your ability to maintain attention and to remember, and learn how to learn.

- Making associations, using mnemonic devices, and grouping information can help improve memory for names and dates. Always carry a small notepad to write down new information that you want to remember.

- Making up a story about items on a list boosts short-term memory. Similarly, if you form mental images of things, you will find it easier to remember. Place important items so that you'll see them when you need them.

- Develop a schedule and a routine to help you remember things you need to do. Always carry your schedule with you and review it regularly. Post reminders where you will see them.

- You can apply special techniques to several other areas of learning:

    Improve your reading comprehension by surveying the material, formulating questions, reading, putting the material into your own words, and then reviewing the material.

    Develop your own system for taking notes.

    Form a project or study group when you can.

    Work with a tutor on difficult material.

11

Social Skills:

Improve Relationships with Others by Improving Knowledge of Yourself

Some adults with ADD excel in social situations. Their high energy and willingness to try new experiences make them vibrant and exciting. ADDers often have a good sense of humor, too, and can think imaginatively. They also are usually good at thinking on their feet. When these skills are present, an ADDer can be charismatic. ADDers do well in sales, public relations, politics, and show business. On the other hand, the social aspect of situations can cause distress for adults with ADD.

Dave was impulsive and somewhat aggressive as a child. He no longer picks fistfights on the playground, but he can really demolish an opponent in an argument. When anyone disagrees with him, he goes blindly on the defensive. He is a rising star in his medical school class. He's able to think broadly and pull together information for diagnoses when others are stumped. He's drawn to medicine for all the right reasons. He cares about people and believes he can help. But his professors worry about his bedside manner. Dave sometimes doesn't hear his patients talking to him—he's so focused on his own thoughts. He's walked away from patients in midsentence as a new idea for treatment hits him. He has trouble handling sensitive topics with patients, too. He's likely to blurt out the problem and then quickly discuss treatment without stopping to sense a reaction. Dave is bewildered. He can't figure out what he's done this time to get such a hostile reaction. While he loves his work and can see the benefits, he's exhausted at day's end. Drained and frustrated by his own clumsiness, he heads home where life with his wife and infant daughter aren't much better.

We don't know of any case in which the importance of your skills in relating to other people can be minimized. Social skills are essential in academic, work, and personal life. The development of good social skills also is one predictor of success for the ADDer in adult life (along with intelligence, finances, family mental health, and the absence of aggression).

Problems in relating well to others begin in childhood. The ADD child is often rejected by peers for impulsive behavior such as teasing or aggression. ADD children also notice at an early age that they are different from others. They are aware of problems with paying attention in class, controlling temper, and keeping still. This sense of being different can result in isolation. The ADD child may withdraw or act out in frustration. Russell Barkley reports that 75 percent of children with ADD will have significant problems in relating to others as an adult. John Ratey, too, does not underestimate the problems that social situations present for ADDers. He states that problems in school and the workplace are often easier to overcome than the issues faced when dealing with other people.

Dr. Ratey also believes that problems with social interactions are directly linked to the neurobiology of ADD. Recall that ADD is a problem of the frontal lobes where information is sorted out and acted on. Because of the impairment, ADDers have difficulty inhibiting impulses—both in what they say and what they do. Impulsively getting into or out of relationships, blurting out opinions, interrupting, and impatience are some of the impulsive behaviors that cause social problems for the ADDer. ADDers also impulsively judge a person or situation. They may jump to a conclusion without really weighing all the information. Distraction, too, is a problem. The ADDer often has trouble paying attention to conversations and remembering what to say. It's difficult for the ADDer to screen information, particularly in new situations or ones that are highly stimulating. It's hard for the adult with ADD to sort out what is relevant and what's not. As a result, the ADDer may become overstimulated and shut down, withdrawing from the social interaction.

Social situations have generated punishment for most adults with ADD. Negative feedback about interrupting, bluntness, excessive talking, and so on, are familiar experiences. Some ADDers, particularly those with hyperactivity, may respond to all of this punishment with aggression or a wild "I don't care" attitude. ADDers without hyperactivity are more likely to withdraw from similar situations and anxiety may arise. Some studies report that 12 percent of adults with ADD are at risk for social phobia—an extreme fear of being embarrassed or humiliated in public. Such fear can lead to avoidance of social situations. The ADDer may then feel isolated and depressed.

We are, by nature, social animals. Difficulty in relating to others can cost the ADDer dearly in happiness, opportunity, and self-esteem. Fortunately, effective social behavior is a skill—or set of skills—that can be developed. Awareness of your personal areas of difficulty and a plan to improve them are the first two steps. A commitment to practicing these new skills and support from others will make the final difference.

Saying No, Saying Yes, and Meaning It

Lynn Weiss writes that adults with ADD often automatically say no. Feeling bombarded with information that can't be sorted out, ADDers blurt out, "No" to seemingly simple requests. The goal is to stop the overstimulation. They do not really mean no. In fact, ADDers often have difficulty saying no and meaning it. When someone asks for help, or a project is announced at work, the ADDer typically volunteers.

1. Do I often feel I have too many projects to complete? Yes _____ No _____

2. Do I often agree to help someone even though I know I don't have the time?
   Yes _____ No _____

3. Do I regret saying yes a lot of the time because I wanted to say no? Yes _____
   No _____

As an adult with ADD, you may have experienced a lot of failure and disappointment saying yes. Offering to help gives you a chance to feel valued—needed. Impulsivity drives this urge to say yes. Often the word is out of your mouth before you think about what you are saying. The result of this willingness to help is a feeling of being overwhelmed with all there is to do and a dread that it can't be done. You end up not completing projects and letting others down. Then the feeling of failure returns—the very emotion to be avoided.

Saying no when you mean it and yes when you mean it will take practice. The habit of volunteering is well established, and you'll need time to change. To ease the burden of turning someone down, try saying, "I'd like to help your project. It is really worthwhile. But I can't commit myself to anything more right now." By acknowledging the person's work, you have extended yourself but not taken on more than you can really handle.

It's also possible to extract yourself from overcommitment before you find you can't complete what you've promised. As soon as you find yourself regretting your impulsive willingness to help, contact the person and explain that it seemed like a good idea when you agreed to it, but now you realize you won't be able to participate after all. While backing out may seem hard to do, it's a lot harder not to be able to complete a project that others are counting on.

Asking for What You Want

Social relationships, whether they are casual friends or closest family members, are based on communication. Letting others know what you need or want is an important part of your

Think of some project you have agreed to do but now realize you can't possibly complete before it's due. How can you explain your need to back out at this time?

_____

Imagine that someone is asking you to do something for them but you can't spare the time. How might you refuse the request?

_____

contribution to communication. ADDers may have trouble expressing their needs. An adult with ADD is often externally oriented. So much time and energy is spent attending to the outside world that the ADDer may never look internally to know personal needs. Being easily overstimulated can also leave adults with ADD overwhelmed and confused about feelings. In exasperation, they may shut down, leave the situation, and never communicate on a really personal level.

1. Do I feel misunderstood a lot of the time? Yes _____ No _____

2. Do I feel frustrated that others can't tell when I need to be alone and when I need to be sociable? Yes _____ No _____

3. Do I sometimes search for words to try to describe how I feel? Yes _____ No _____

Communicating your needs is a two-step process. First, identify what you want. If you can't identify your needs in the frustration of the moment, ask for some time to think. If you still have trouble finding the feelings, choose a direction and go with it for a while. You'll be able to tell if it's right for you.

The second step in the communication process is to clearly state what you want to others. It's important at this point to use *I*. For example, if it's just expected that you'll meet family or friends at a standing day and time, you need to make a clear statement, such as, "I want to make some other plans this week." Similarly, if your friends are pressuring you to drink and you are determined to quit, you need to make an *I* statement such as, "I'm not interested. I'm quitting." While you may get resistance initially, over time people will develop a respect for your ability to act on your own.

Here is another example: If you really want to go out for the evening, say, "I'd like to go out tonight." If you ask, "What do you want to do tonight?" you're less likely to get your needs met or even acknowledged. Others, of course, are not always going to agree with you, but by asking, you'll at least create the opportunity to negotiate.

Think of an upcoming situation with a friend or family member. How will you ask for what you want in this situation? _____

_____

Keeping Promises

Overcommitment and difficulty saying no may cause ADDers to break promises. Naturally, they feel bad about letting others down and failing again. Those who are disappointed begin to lose their trust, and relationships are strained. Another reason for breaking promises is inattention. The ADDer may get distracted by some interesting project and just forget to be somewhere on time. The person left waiting feels devalued and a bit miffed. The problem is made worse by the fact that the ADDer seems to be able to remember other appointments without a problem. Again, the disappointed person feels it's a personal insult, feels devalued, and angry.

1. Am I aware that I break promises or just let others down frequently? Yes _____ No _____

2. Do others occasionally say to me when I make a promise, "I'll believe it when I see it" or "I've heard that before"? Yes _____ No _____

Keeping your word is important to maintaining relationships. It's necessary to learn to say no and to take on only those commitments that you really want to keep. Then you need to use your daily or weekly planner to keep track of your promises. You must take them as seriously as other work or personal commitments. If you do break a promise, talk to the person you've let down. Explain what happened. Apologize and ask if there is a way you can make amends.

List promises you have made to others lately: _____

_____

Schedule time to complete these tasks in your daily/weekly planner.

Listening Skills

Comments such as, "You never hear a word I say" are familiar to most adults with ADD. ADDers often have poor listening skills due to the nature of the disorder. Distractibility interferes with good listening. If you are noticing everything going on around you, you're likely to miss parts of conversations. Restlessness also interferes. Fidgeting and difficulty staying still feed into distractibility and make good listening unlikely. Impulsivity, too, plays a role in poor listening. The urge to interrupt, change the subject, or blurt out some opinion also disrupts the listening process.

1. Do others often tell me that I am not listening? Yes _____ No _____

2. Do I have trouble concentrating when others speak? Yes _____ No _____

3. Do I find that I have missed parts of conversations? Yes _____ No _____

To improve your listening skills, you need to take a more active role in the process. Ask questions of the speaker. By formulating questions, you are keeping your mind actively involved in the topic, and you're less likely to be distracted. If you are in a lecture environment, formulate questions even if you can't ask them. Make frequent eye contact with the speaker. This will help reduce distractibility. If you can, do your listening in a place that is low in distraction—close the door, meet away from phones, or in a restaurant, sit facing the wall. When you feel you've reached your limit for listening, take a break from the interaction. Resume when you feel ready.

Interrupting

Interrupting is one of the most frequent complaints ADDers hear from others. Interrupting is a form of impulsivity. The ADDer has difficulty waiting patiently for a break in the conversation. ADDers report that they worry they'll forget what they have to say, so they break

Exercise

Meet with someone for a casual conversation. Implement techniques to improve your listening skills. When you note improvement, meet with someone who does not interest you and practice listening well even when your motivation is low.

1. Have others told me that I tend to interrupt them when they're speaking? Yes _____ No _____

2. Have I noticed others looking surprised or angered when I break into a conversation? Yes _____ No _____

in when the thought occurs. If you've been interrupted, especially in the middle of some topic of concern to you, then you know how maddening this can be.

You can use several techniques to stop the bad habit of interrupting others. Ask someone to give you a signal when you interrupt others. If you do interrupt, stop as soon as you realize your mistake. By stopping yourself, you weaken the interrupting response and make it less likely to occur in the future. When you stop your interruption, you can use humor or apologize to others and ask to return to the original topic.

Exercise

Ask a friend to talk at length about a topic you care about very much. Practice not interrupting. Repeat the exercise until you can participate in a twenty-minute conversation without interrupting.

Being Blunt

Closely related to interrupting is the habit of blurting out opinions before thinking. Like interrupting, being blunt is impulsive behavior. It is having a thought and acting on it before thinking. This impulsive behavior usually causes embarrassment for the speaker and the recipient. Typically what is said is a comment that over- or understates the situation. Often the comments are meant to be funny but somehow fall flat in the open air.

---

1. Do I catch myself sometimes speaking before I think? Yes _____ No _____

2. Have I noticed a surprised look on the faces of others when I say things? Yes _____ No _____

3. Have others told me that they're "surprised" at what I say? Yes _____ No _____

You are most likely to be blunt when you're under pressure, anxious, or overstimulated. When you feel yourself really speeding up, take a break, slow down, and then rejoin others. If you are very blunt, be sure to acknowledge your behavior. It's tempting to ignore what you've said as if it doesn't matter. But if feelings are hurt, regain control by remarking on the behavior. Try to smooth things over with humor or an apology.

Exercise

Monitor yourself closely at the next staff meeting or social gathering. Remind yourself to slow down and take breaks as needed. Keep count of the times you stopped yourself from impulsive speech. Give yourself a pat on the back or something special for the control you showed.

Being Abrupt

Adults with ADD are often thought to be rude. Interrupting, bluntness, and being abrupt all lend ammunition to this charge. ADDers have a low tolerance for frustration. They may abruptly hang up the phone when angry or walk away from a disagreement. ADDers become so frustrated that they can't think, and they feel compelled to escape the overwhelming emotion. This abruptness naturally stimulates some angry feelings in the recipient. If not carefully resolved, hard feelings can endure.

As always, developing an awareness of your behavior patterns is the first step in breaking a bad habit. Be aware of your rising frustration level. Before you get to the boiling point, take control of your feelings. Tell the other person that you are feeling angry and

1. Have I hung up the phone or walked away from someone in frustration lately?
Yes _____ No _____

2. Do I sometimes feel so frustrated that I can't even think? Yes _____ No _____

frustrated and can't talk further now; that you'll call later when you feel able to discuss the point rationally. If you do impulsively end an interaction, be sure to contact the person later, explain what you were feeling, and apologize if needed.

Exercise

The next time you need to contact a utility company, the Department of Motor Vehicles, or another bureaucratic institution, spend five minutes preparing for the interaction. Remind yourself to be aware of your frustration level, and prepare to handle your mounting anger.

Talking Too Much

While ADDers may listen too little, they often talk too much. Poor listening may be the result of inattention due to distractibility. Talking too much is fostered by the opposite experience—hyperfocusing. Ironically, ADDers often have the special ability to concentrate deeply on a topic of interest. This interest can be translated into an enthusiasm for talking—sometimes at length—on a subject.

1. Have others told me that I talk too much? Yes _____ No _____

2. Do others often excuse themselves and leave a conversation with me? Yes _____ No _____

In normal conversation, each speaker tends to talk for up to twenty seconds at a time. Try to keep this rough time limit in mind when talking—particularly on a topic that interests you greatly. Look for the nonverbal behavior of others. If others begin to look around, look at their watches, an so forth, you've talked too long. Also, ask questions of your audience. If they have questions about what you're saying, they are probably interested in the topic, too. If they don't have questions or say something noncommittal, such as "That's interesting," you've likely lost them. If you're not sure about their response, feel free to ask them if this is interesting to them.

Exercise

Begin a conversation with a friend on a topic you really care about. Observe your friend's reactions to the topic. What nonverbal social cues can you read? Is your friend asking questions? Try to keep your speech to about twenty seconds at a time.

Committing to a Relationship

Mental and physical restlessness can interfere with the ADDer's ability to make commitments. An ADDer often pursues a relationship with enthusiasm. However, all too soon the novelty wears off, and the ADDer looks for interesting experiences elsewhere. This pattern of brief but intense relationships can leave the adult with ADD with few real friends, and deep, committed relationships can never develop. The pattern is particularly destructive if a marriage is involved. ADDers do have a higher divorce rate than adults without this disorder. It is often the aftermath of a divorce that brings the ADDer to counseling for the first time, and the ADDer may, with luck, be diagnosed.

ADDers often confuse the person with the event. That is, if the event feels a little stale, such as a party or movie, the ADDer may feel it's the person they're with. Similarly, if they're enthusiastic about someone, the person may be taking on the characteristics of a highly interesting environment. It can be difficult for the ADDer to see someone independent of the current setting. To break this pattern, you need to be aware that you may be blurring the lines between person and environment. Stop and ask yourself if you are really growing bored with a person or just the activities you choose.

1. Have I had many brief friendships with people? Yes _____ No _____

2. Do I have any friendships that have lasted several years? Yes _____ No _____

3. Do I feel restless in a relationship after a few weeks or months? Yes _____ No _____

Exercise

If you are experiencing restlessness in a friendship or other relationship, think of the last three times you felt this way. Next, remember what you were doing at those times. Was it the person or the event that left you feeling bored?

Reading Social Cues

ADDers miss a lot of useful information by not attending to social cues. The ADDer's mind, and sometimes body, is typically going too fast to pay attention to the tone of voice, facial expression, and body language of others. Distractions also play a role in missing social information. ADDers may be thinking of a conversation across the room and miss a great deal of what's going on under their noses.

1. Am I aware of how others stand, look, and sound when I interact with them?
   Yes _____ No _____

2. Have I used information from the body language, tone of voice, and facial expression of others, to understand an interaction? Yes _____ No _____

Once treatment for ADD begins, many adults are amazed at the information they have missed in not really attending to the behavior of others. They often report seeing friends and family having strong emotional reactions for the first time. This information, once attended to, can be used to guide and improve communication.

Exercise

Go to a public place where there are many people (shopping mall, airport, library, for example) and observe someone for a few minutes. Be careful not to stare. Look at the face and identify the emotion expressed. Look at the body posture—what is being communicated? Repeat this practice until you can get a feeling for someone's nonverbal communication within a few seconds.

With so many things to focus on, learning to pay attention to nonverbal information may sound like an impossiblility. But increased awareness will lend results. Remember that skills in any area aren't built in a day. Practice is the key to improvement.

Keeping Pace with Companions

ADDers, particularly those with hyperactivity, look to the rest of the world like they're going a mile a minute. Even without hyperactivity, adults with ADD may be restless or have bouts of high energy. When in high gear, the ADDer may talk excessively fast. Physical restlessness and the urge to be moving is common, too. Others may interpret this amount of motion as like boredom. Fidgeting, rushing through a conversation, and even just leaving the room may be perceived as insulting to others. The ADDer may, of course, be very interested in the person or conversation, but just have difficulty controlling a physical drive.

1. Have others told me that I talk very fast? Yes _____ No _____

2. Have others asked me to slow down, that they can't keep up? Yes _____ No _____

3. Am I aware of talking or moving faster than others typically do? Yes _____ No _____

To make sure you're not leaving others behind, watch for social cues. When people begin to look tired or frustrated while being with you, you know you're out of sync. Ask for feedback. If you're zipping through a shopping mall or hardware store with someone, you may need to take some breaks from each other or take a break together in a quiet area. Cue yourself to slow down. It can feel good to let off the brakes and go at top speed, but do it alone or with another high-energy person. Finally, fidget quietly. Have some object handy (a pen for example) to twirl when confined to a place, so that you can expend some extra energy in a nondisruptive way.

Exercise

Set up an audiotape (or videotape) in a situation at home in which you will be interacting with people. Play the tape back and see if you are talking/moving at high speed. Observe the behavior of others. Do they look overwhelmed or exasperated at your speed?

Practicing Patience

Most people hate to wait, but ADDers can be particularly impatient. ADDers are anxious to get on to the next thing and usually "just want to get this over with." Standing in line can be uncomfortable, too. ADDers often feel overly confined and rebel against the uniformity of a line. The frustration of waiting may be too much, and the ADDer may bolt from the situation just to release tension.

1. Do I avoid situations where I may have to wait even short periods of time? Yes _____ No _____

2. Do I particularly dislike standing in a line? Yes _____ No _____

3. Do I often leave a situation if I'll have to wait for any period of time? Yes _____ No _____

Time spent waiting can be put to good use. First, it's necessary to stop the flood of negative emotion that may accompany waiting. Tell yourself that it's OK, time will pass, you can stand the wait. Then you can use your waiting time to plan—dinner for that night or what you're going to do next weekend. Many ADDers carry books or crossword puzzles with them just to see them through waiting time. Finally, relax. It's a good opportunity to practice deep breathing—and imagery.

Exercise

Put together a plan for yourself to tolerate waiting. Remind yourself to be patient—that you can tolerate the wait. What activity will you do to bridge the time you have to wait?

_____

_____

If you're going to take a book or puzzle, buy it now and put it in a pocket or purse to be handy.

Being Honest

From an early age, ADDers feel different. They're aware that sitting still and paying attention are difficult for them. When differences are noticed by other children, the child with ADD can take some rough teasing. To avoid these bad experiences, ADDers begin a lifelong effort to cover up perceived flaws.

One troublesome attempt to hide the symptoms of ADD is the tendency to lie. A number of researchers report on the frequency of lying and identify reasons for it. ADDers often lie in order to cover up a poor memory. Rather than admitting they forgot a birthday, they'll launch into a long explanation of being sick or overworked. Lying temporarily helps to avoid embarrassment for a very human experience of forgetting. ADDers also tend to miss parts of conversations. To cover up their mental absences, they may make up information they need to pass on. While lies are attempts to avoid immediate pain of embarrassment, they tend to fail in the long run. Being a good liar requires a good memory since it's necessary to remember what stories you've told.

1. Do I often tell lies to cover up a mistake I've made? Yes _____ No _____

2. Do I sometimes lie even when the truth really isn't so bad? Yes _____ No _____

3. Have I gotten feedback from others about not telling the truth? Yes _____ No _____

Overcoming lying is a two-step process. It's important to come to terms with many aspects of ADD, such as problems with memory. When you accept that you have a problem, you'll be less inclined to hide it and your motivation to lie will diminish. A second step is to break the habit. Adults with ADD have been hiding themselves for a long time. Lying may be automatic by now. To break the habit, prompt yourself to tell the truth. Remind yourself that the truth is easier in the long run. If you do lie, admit the truth as soon as possible. This is painful to do, but it will make lying far less attractive in the future.

Exercise

Think of a lie you've told recently. Contact the person involved and admit the truth. You don't need to explain your behavior unless you want to.

Showing Consideration and Compassion for Others

ADDers are often called selfish. To others, ADDers live in a private world. They seem to focus well on personally interesting topics, but have difficulty attending to others' needs and interests. The ADDer also remembers personally important information while forgetting things valued by friends and family. In addition, the ADD adult may react impulsively to situations without noticing the feelings of others. The conclusion, largely inaccurate, is that the ADDer doesn't care about others.

1. Do others tell me that I'm selfish or insensitive? Yes _____ No _____

2. Do I feel that I have been neglecting friends and family for my own pursuits?
Yes _____ No _____

We know, though, that ADDers can be very compassionate individuals. Overcoming the perceptions of others involves a complex, multistep approach: Medication is very often effective in getting yourself to slow down and to focus on others. Counseling can be helpful, too, in learning to see your behavior from a different perspective. Finally, when you are ready, you must make the effort to notice what those around you are feeling and needing to communicate to you.

Exercise

Choose a friend or family member you have been neglecting lately. Make the effort to pay attention to conversation, interests, and his or her needs.

Summary

- Some adults with ADD excel at social situations; others are distressed by the demand to pay attention, think before acting, and manage restlessness. These problems begin in childhood when the ADDer identifies a need to cover up impulses resulting from the disorder.

- Problems in social skills are directly related to impulsivity, inattention, and hyperactivity of ADD. The areas addressed in this chapter that ADDers have trouble with include:

Saying no or yes and meaning it	Asking for what you want
Reading social cues	Keeping promises
Listening skills	Being honest
Committing to relationship	Considering others

- Problems with social skills are difficult to master because each social situation is unique and requires flexible application of what you know.

12

Final Points:

Do You Want to Tell Others You Have ADD?

You've probably experienced the urge to tell family, teachers, and co-workers about your diagnosis of ADD. You may have tested the waters. Reactions to your announcement can be extremely varied. Even people you would credit with enlightened opinions can scoff and call it a fad or an excuse. Others may be interested, curious, and concerned.

Deciding when to tell others about ADD is a personal decision. There are a few factors you may want to consider before moving ahead:

- It's important to feel comfortable with your knowledge of ADD. Be aware of what problems are associated with ADD. Also, you'll need to know what treatments are used for these problems. Many well-meaning people will want to give you advice. They may tell you to skip medication—you don't need it. Or you may be advised to follow a sugar-free diet or take extra vitamins—neither of which has been found to offset ADD symptoms. You'll want to feel confident in your handling of ADD so that you don't go down a blind alley.

- Feel confident in your diagnosis. Know which of your problems are related to ADD and which are not. It's tempting to think that every issue you face is a result of ADD, but that may not be the case. Particularly if you've had a childhood disrupted by divorce, abuse, or physical illness, you'll need to work with a therapist to sort out your ADD issues from other life experiences.

- Be sure you're ready for any reaction. Even people who are knowledgeable about medical and psychological issues may know very little about ADD. You may be surprised at their reaction. You're likely to tell others about your ADD because you need their understanding and support. Instead you may get a raised eyebrow, disheartened sigh, and a lecture on "what's really ailing you." Again, be prepared. You don't want to take negative reactions personally. Don't let others shake your belief in what you're doing.

- Be sure of your motivation for telling others about your ADD. It's important for you, too, not to use ADD as an excuse for unacceptable behavior or to expect others to help you in ways you could help yourself. You may need to tell others about ADD if it will help them to understand what *you* are trying to do to help yourself and if you need them to assist or accommodate you in this effort.

Telling Family and Friends About Your ADD

Those closest to you are likely to be the ones you first want to tell about your ADD diagnosis. If you're living with them, it will probably be no surprise. After all, they've seen your mood swings, unfinished projects, and frustration with these problems. Still, family and friends may be uneducated about ADD and skeptical of the diagnosis. As always, you need to prepare for any reaction.

If you feel your relationships can benefit from disclosing ADD, then the effort may be worth it. Find a quiet time when you can concentrate and spend some time talking. Be sure to tell others why you are disclosing your ADD to them. Tell them what you hope their reaction will be and what you'll need from them as you continue to master ADD symptoms. You may find that one conversation isn't enough. Others may need some time to mull it over and then ask more questions. Realize that accepting your ADD is a process for others. It will take some time for them to really grasp it.

Exercise

This exercise will help you decide whether to tell family and friends about your ADD.

1. Do I feel ready to talk about ADD with a friend or family member? Yes _____ No _____

2. Who would I like to tell first, second, etc.? _____

3. When is a good time to talk about it? _____

4. What reaction am I expecting? _____

5. What help will I ask for? _____

Letting People Know at School and Work

You may wonder whether you should tell teachers, co-workers, or employers about ADD. Again, this is a very personal decision—one you'll want to reach after much thought and weighing both the pros and cons of your decision. We advise not to tell people outside your close circle of family and friends. You can ask for accommodations without telling of your diagnosis. For example, at work you may be able to tell your supervisor that your office is noisy and full of distractions and that you could do better work if you moved to a quieter space. At school, you may be able to tell your teacher that you have trouble remembering assignments that are given orally and ask for the assignment to be written.

If you have tried to ask for what you need in an informal way without disclosing your ADD and you are still at risk for failing, in school or work, you may decide to meet with your teacher or supervisor. As always, prepare yourself for any reaction. Be clear why you are revealing your ADD and be clear in what you want to ask for in assistance.

You also may want to become familiar with the Americans with Disabilities Act (ADA) passed by Congress in 1990. The ADA applies to a workplace employing more than fifteen people. ADA classifies ADD as a disability if it significantly interferes with your ability to do your job. You must have first shown that you are qualified for the job by meeting any educational standard and demonstrating that you can perform the work. You must also show good work habits, such as working required hours, arriving on time, and being responsive to other standards of performance set by the employer. Under these circumstances, the employer is required to provide reasonable accommodations for your disability. The courts have yet to decide what "reasonable accommodations" means. Some ideas include

- Assist in reducing distractions when possible
- Provide very clear instructions on work assignments
- Help to establish short-term deadlines for projects
- Provide instructions in writing
- Review work and performance at frequent intervals
- Assist in setting priorities
- Provide assistance with clerical work

Conclusion

You've come a long way and worked through the major symptoms of inattention, impulsivity, and hyperactivity. You've also addressed mood swings, depression, anxiety, self-esteem, social and learning skills. It's taken perseverance on your part to get this far. But perseverance is not a stranger to adults with ADD. For most of your life you've had to find ways to cope, even in the absence of understanding and support from others. With the information you have now, you can put your perseverance to work in a more goal-directed way.

Exercise

Do this exercise to help decide whether to discuss your ADD with people at work or school.

1. Am I encountering problems in school or work related to my ADD? Yes _____
   No _____

2. What accommodations do I need to ask for?

   a. _____

   b. _____

   c. _____

   d. _____

3. Can I ask for accommodations without discussing ADD? Yes _____ No _____

4. If I need to discuss my ADD with my teachers or employer, how will I present it?

   _____

Even though you're actively involved in learning about ADD and changing old habits for new ones, it's important to accept yourself. It's important to understand that your old ways of coping were what you could do at the time. Realize that everyone—with and without ADD—has limits and can only do so much at any one time. Be kind to yourself, and forgive yourself and others as you work toward making life better.

Choose to be around people who are supportive of you. You don't need or deserve unkindness. Some people feel that negative reactions stimulate and motivate them, but in the long run, criticism hurts. Find people who have a positive approach to life and who are interested and care about you. Finally, be willing to learn new ways of dealing with ADD. You'll appreciate the relief you get with improved coping skills. You deserve the improved relationships and increased opportunities you can find.

Summary

• Telling others that you have ADD is a personal decision. Before revealing your ADD:

   Be comfortable in your knowledge of ADD.

   Feel confident in your diagnosis.

   Be sure of your motivation for telling others.

- You may feel the urge to tell family and friends as well as people at work or school. In general, it is much better to seek accommodations at work or school rather than reveal your diagnosis.

- While learning and changing, it's important to accept yourself. You're a human being who is learning and doing as much as you can at the present time. Choose to be around people who are interested and care about you, and above all, keep trying.

Bibliography

Barkely, R. A. *Hyperactive Children: A Handbook for Diagnosis and Treatment.* New York: Guilford, 1981.

Beck, A. T. *Cognitive Therapy and Emotional Disorders.* New York: New American Library, 1979.

Davis, M., E. R. Eshelman, and M. McKay. *The Relaxation & Stress Reduction Workbook.* Oakland, CA: New Harbinger Publications, 1988.

Hallowell, E. D., and J. J. Ratey. *Driven to Distraction.* New York: Random House, 1994.

———. *Anwers to Distraction.* New York: Pantheon Books, 1994.

Kelly, K., and P. Ramundo. *You Mean I'm Not Lazy, Stupid or Crazy.* New York: Scribner, 1995.

Kubler-Ross, Elizabeth. *On Death and Dying.* New York: Alfred A. Dnopf, 1981.

McKay, M., and P. Fanning. *Self-Esteem.* Oakland, CA: New Harbinger Publications, 1987.

McKay, M., P. D. Rogers, and J. McKay. *When Anger Hurts.* Oakland, CA: New Harbinger Publications, 1989.

Murphy, K. R., and S. LeVert. *Out of the Fog.* New York: Hyperion, 1995.

Nadeau, K. G. *A Comprehensive Guide to Attention Deficit Disorder in Adults.* New York: Brunner/Mazel, 1995.

Plante, T. G. "Psychological Benefits of Exercise." *Healthline 14* (1995): 3–4.

Premack, D. "Toward Empirical Behavioral Laws: Positive Reinforcement" *Psychological Review 66* (1959):219–233.

Prochaska, J. O., J. C. Norcross, and C. C. DiClemente. *Changing for Good.* New York: William Morrow and Company, 1994.

Roberts, M. S. *Living Without Procrastination.* Oakland, CA: New Harbinger Publications, 1995.

Solden, S. *Women with Attention Deficit Disorder.* Grass Valley, CA: Underwood Books, 1995.

Whileman, T. A., M. Novotni, and P. Peterson. *Adult ADD.* Colorado Springs: Pinon Press, 1995.

Zametkin, A. J., T. E. Nordahl, .M. Gross, A. C. King, W. E. Semple, J. Rumsey, S. Hamburger, and R. M. Cohen. "Cerebral Glucose Metabolism in Adults with Hyperactivity of Childhood Onset." *New England Journal of Medicine 323* (1990): 1361–1366.

Some Other
New Harbinger Titles

Angry All the Time, Item 3929 $13.95

Handbook of Clinical Psychopharmacology for Therapists, 4th edition, Item 3996 $55.95

Writing For Emotional Balance, Item 3821 $14.95

Surviving Your Borderline Parent, Item 3287 $14.95

When Anger Hurts, 2nd edition, Item 3449 $16.95

Calming Your Anxious Mind, Item 3384 $12.95

Ending the Depression Cycle, Item 3333 $17.95

Your Surviving Spirit, Item 3570 $18.95

Coping with Anxiety, Item 3201 $10.95

The Agoraphobia Workbook, Item 3236 $19.95

Loving the Self-Absorbed, Item 3546 $14.95

Transforming Anger, Item 352X $10.95

Don't Let Your Emotions Run Your Life, Item 3090 $17.95

Why Can't I Ever Be Good Enough, Item 3147 $13.95

Your Depression Map, Item 3007 $19.95

Successful Problem Solving, Item 3023 $17.95

Working with the Self-Absorbed, Item 2922 $14.95

The Procrastination Workbook, Item 2957 $17.95

Coping with Uncertainty, Item 2965 $11.95

The BDD Workbook, Item 2930 $18.95

You, Your Relationship, and Your ADD, Item 299X $17.95

The Stop Walking on Eggshells Workbook, Item 2760 $18.95

Conquer Your Critical Inner Voice, Item 2876 $15.95

The PTSD Workbook, Item 2825 $17.95

Hypnotize Yourself Out of Pain Now!, Item 2809 $14.95

The Depression Workbook, 2nd edition, Item 268X $19.95

Beating the Senior Blues, Item 2728 $17.95

Shared Confinement, Item 2663 $15.95

Getting Your Life Back Together When You Have Schizophrenia, Item 2736 $14.95

Do-It-Yourself Eye Movement Technique for Emotional Healing, Item 2566 $13.95

Call **toll free, 1-800-748-6273,** or log on to our online bookstore at **www.newharbinger.com** to order. Have your Visa or Mastercard number ready. Or send a check for the titles you want to New Harbinger Publications, Inc., 5674 Shattuck Ave., Oakland, CA 94609. Include $4.50 for the first book and 75¢ for each additional book, to cover shipping and handling. (California residents please include appropriate sales tax.) Allow two to five weeks for delivery.

Prices subject to change without notice.

U.S. $18.95

Self-Help/Health

LIVING WITH
ADD

A Workbook for Adults with Attention Deficit Disorder

Attention Deficit Disorder is a little-understood brain imbalance that usually manifests itself as childhood hyperactivity. Although the syndrome is harder to recognize in adults, pyschiatrists who specialize in the disorder estimate that it may affect between three to ten million people in the United States alone.

This interactive workbook enables readers who are struggling with the condition to identify the personal problems caused by it and develop skills for coping with them. Readers learn how to assess themselves and work through exercises structured to help them deal with self-esteem issues, change negative or distorted thinking patterns, manage stress, and develop a structured approach to starting and finishing tasks. Final chapters offer specific suggestions for handling common problems at work and school, dealing with intimate relationships, and finding support.

M. Susan Roberts, Ph.D., is a behavioral psychologist for South Shore Mental Health Center and clinical director of the Emergency Services Inpatient Unit at Fuller Hospital, in Attleboro, Massachusetts. She is the author of *Living Without Procrastination*.

Gerard J. Jansen, Ph.D., is a financial analyst with a major software company in the Boston area.

Cover design by Lightbourne Images.

NEW HARBINGER
PUBLICATIONS, INC.

9 781572 240636   51895

ISBN 1-57224-063-6